EXPERIENCE VS. UNDERSTANDING

EXPERIENCE VS. UNDERSTANDING

Understanding Yourself in Twenty-First Century Societies

HARRY C. BREDEMEIER

Routledge
Taylor & Francis Group
LONDON AND NEW YORK

First published 1998 by Transaction Publishers
Arrangement with Janus Publishing Company.

Published 2017 by Routledge
2 Park Square, Milton Park, Abingdon, Oxon OX14 4RN
711 Third Avenue, New York, NY 10017

First issued in paperback 2018

Routledge is an imprint of the Taylor and Francis Group, an informa business

Copyright © 1998 by Harry C. Bredemeier.

All rights reserved. No part of this book may be reprinted or reproduced or utilised in any form or by any electronic, mechanical, or other means, now known or hereafter invented, including photocopying and recording, or in any information storage or retrieval system, without permission in writing from the publishers.

Notice:
Product or corporate names may be trademarks or registered trademarks, and are used only for identification and explanation without intent to infringe.

Library of Congress Catalog Number: 98-9739

Library of Congress Cataloging-in-Publication Data

Bredemeier, Harry Charles.
    Experience vs. understanding : understanding yourself in twenty-first century societies / Harry C. Bredemeier.
       p. cm.
    Originally published : London : Janus Pub. Co., 1997.
    Includes bibliographical references.
    ISBN 0-7658-0446-8 (cloth : alk. paper)
    1. Social psychology. 2. Social perception. 3. Social ethics.
4. Experience. 5. Comprehension. I. Title.
HM251.B626   1998   98-9739
302—dc21   CIP

ISBN 13: 978-1-138-50994-8 (pbk)
ISBN 13: 978-0-7658-0446-4 (hbk)

The Statue: What I was going to ask Juan was why Life should bother itself about getting a brain. Why should it want to understand itself? Why not be content to enjoy itself?

Don Juan: Without a brain, Commander, you would enjoy yourself without knowing it, and so lose all the fun.

The Statue: True, most true. But I am quite content with brain enough to know that I'm enjoying myself. I don't want to understand why. In fact, I'd rather not. My experience is that one's pleasures don't bear thinking about.

Don Juan: That is why intellect is so unpopular. But to Life, the force behind the man, intellect is a necessity, because without it he blunders into death. Just as Life, after ages of struggle, evolved that wonderful bodily organ the eye, so that the living organism could see where it was going and what was coming to help or threaten it, and thus avoid a thousand dangers that formerly slew it, so it is evolving today a mind's eye that shall see ... the purpose of Life, and thereby enable the individual to work for that purpose instead of thwarting and baffling it by setting up shortsighted personal aims as at present.

George Bernard Shaw, *Man and Superman*, Act III

A rational environmental movement cannot be built on the demand to save the environment ... Remaking the world is the universal property of living organisms and is inextricably bound up with their nature. Rather, we must decide what kind of world we want to live in and then try to manage the processes of change as best we can to approximate it.

R C Lewontin, 'Genes, Environments, And Organisms' in Robert B Silvers (ed), *Hidden Histories of Science*, New York Review Book, 1995.

For Mary, for everything
And Myrna, who chanted

Contents

The chapter outlines in this table of contents are the summaries of each chapter which are also provided at its conclusion.

Preface   xv

Part 1   Actions and Consequences   1

1   The Interpretation of Experience   3

Experience Is Not a Good Teacher

The Need for Interpretation – and Testing
All experiences, from sunrises to crime and taxes, require cultural interpretation; and the interpretations require testing.

Knowledge, Choice and Responsibility
If you have knowledge of alternatives and their consequences, you are responsible for the consequences of your choices.

Two Metaphors: the Titanic *and Smallpox*
Great danger lies in not thinking beyond immediate perceptions.

Summary

Experience versus Understanding

2 The First Choice: Deciding What It Is All For   13

Evaluation and Purpose
You cannot evaluate anything without a conception of what it is for.

What Are People For?
People may be conceived as for themselves or for any of several other kinds of things.

The Limits on the Parts of the Whole
An iron law of systems constrains choices: subsystems must not further their subsystem welfare at the expense of the system.

Appendix

The Tragedy of the Commons

Prisoners' Dilemma

Summary

3 The Welfare of the Species and the Shaping of Behaviour   25

Cultural Requirements for Human Welfare
The long-term welfare of the human species requires effective moral rules for the pursuit of understanding, of technological coping, of justice, and of art; and those rules require certain kinds of people.

Shaping Human Behaviour
We become the people we are through a basic principle of evolution: internal controls lead to actions which environments differentially select for survival.

Knowledge and Responsibility
Once we know the ways people are shaped, we become responsible for how people are shaped, if we have power.

Contents

Ecclesiastes

Summary

4 Why We Act As We Do   35

The Determinants of Our Decisions
The immediate determinants of our behaviour are the values of eleven variables inside us, often referred to as 'character' or 'free will'.

Experiences as Determinants
The major determinants of those internal controls are experiences prescribed and interpreted by culture.

Culture as Determinant
All human activities are governed by cultural rules stating nine critical elements illustrated by the rules of baseball.

Cultural Games as Mazes
Consequently, the institutional games of life are homologous to the mazes causing laboratory animals to run the paths they run.

Scripts, Decisions and Actions
The immediate reason the values of our decision variable are what they are is that that is what the cultural scripts governing us say they should be.

Summary

5 Power, Behaviour, and Success   51

The Nature of Power
Power is the probability of getting others to act as one wants them to act; and five variables determine how much one has.

Game Scripts and Power
The values of those variables are also determined by the cultural scripts of the institutional games of life.

Experience versus Understanding

Power and Mattering
Mattering in human life, and power, come to the same thing.

Bargaining Power
An important difference between power and bargaining power is that the more you want something, the greater is your power, other things being equal, and the less your bargaining power.

You Are What Happened to You
A crucial understanding to bring to all experiences is that everyone *is* the result of his or her experiences in prior cultural games.

Your Behaviour and Power: Yours and Others
The relation between your power and other people's is a major determinant of you and your actions.

Power, Competition, and Performance
Your competitors are related shapers of you.

Understanding and Choice
The more you understand about power, the greater is your responsibility for the consequences of your choices.

Summary

Part 2 Humanism and Individualism: Similarities and Differences   65

6 Virtues and Justice   67

Moral Virtues and Amino Acids
Human beings rely on morals to elicit the society-enhancing behaviour that is elicited in social insects by DNA.

The Insufficiency of Virtues
Individual virtues such as intelligence or courage are not sufficient to evaluate actions; they are common to saints and sinners.

Justice
Justice is the major quality of rules that motivates people to obey them. People think that fairness requires equality of treatments, unless inequality can be justified in terms of equality of respect. A possible justification of unequal treatments is that they result from the same operation of blind chance as prevails in a woodland. Here pure individualism regards human social life as an instance of ecological principles. 'To each according to his ability to benefit those who have the resources to benefit those who benefit them.'

The Humanistic Conception of Justice
Justice requires equality of respect. Fairness prevails when the ratios of people's rewards to their costs and risks are equal. It requires that people be equally empowered, or compensated for unequal empowerments.

Being Honest
The great costs of the individualistic view do not compel humanism; but honesty at least requires their up-front acceptance. An acceptance speech is supplied.

Summary

7 The Problem of Losers

Keeping Losers in the Game
Under rules of individualism, losers pose problems like those of marks in confidence games: how do you keep them from spoiling the game?

The Humanistic Interpretation: Assurance and Insurance
Under humanistic rules, if you cannot assure people of adequate power, your duty is to insure them against the failure. Power is like health: since you might lose it accidentally, insurance makes good sense.

Experience versus Understanding

The Two Traps
It is morally monstrous to encourage powerlessness or to exploit the powerless and it is morally idiotic not to demand of the less powerful what they can contribute.

Determinism and Responsibility
The fact that your behaviour is determined does not mean that you are not responsible for it. Quite the contrary.

Determinism and the Self
Your self was *determined by* the degree to which you were held responsible for your actions.

Summary

8 Culture and Freedom

Freedom and Privilege
Maximizing freedom is an oxymoron: within individuals, freedom is limited by character; between people, freedom is zero-sum.

Markets and Democracies
Markets and democracies are protections against the operation of Lord Acton's dictum that power corrupts. The free market is a set of rules sharply *restricting* people's freedoms. Democratic freedom is a set of rules sharply *limiting* people's freedoms.

People's Wants and Human Needs
That markets and democracies maximize control by consumers and citizens does not necessarily lead to a desirable society.

Freedom and Minorities
The zero sum nature of freedom is nowhere clearer than in the case of minority rights and demands for various freedoms.

Summary

Contents

9 The Preciousness of Persons   121

To Whom Are Persons Precious – and Why?
For humanists, individuals are precious to everyone because they are trustees of the species' gene pool and cultures, and the only audience there is of the human drama.

Some Classical Formulations of Humanism

Saving and Spending Time and Persons
Individuals are like time: they cannot be hoarded; only invested, spent, or wasted.

The Plea of the Ovum
A thought experiment: every ovum pleads to be fertilized and born well, or else aborted.

Key Understandings of Humanism
The intellectual understandings that should, humanistically, guide interpretations of experiences are summarized in a few interrelated propositions.

The Physical and Moral Universes
Viable human societies need to construct a moral universe with principles as implacable as those of the physical universe.

The Impossibility of Not Being a Moral Environment
You cannot avoid being one kind or another of morally selective environment to people around you; but you may be one kind or another.

The Place of Physical Force
In the absence of shared premises, conflict resolution requires either force or divorce – and shared premises must ultimately be backed by force.

Fundamental Conflicts and Ultimate Purposes
When people's conceptions of what they are for consist of subsystems of the species, conflicts are resolvable only by force, if they are resolvable at all.

Summary

Experience versus Understanding

10 Foreign Policy   141

National and Personal Foreign Policy
The issues of national foreign policy parallel those of each person's policy towards other people's.

How Many Lives Should Be Risked?
If individuals are only for themselves, international force cannot be justified; but if they are investable in something else, it can be. But risking lives in war or peace-keeping operations requires weighing the value of investing human life-years for one set of consequences against risking them for another set.

To Whom Do People Owe Duties?
We owe duties to everyone with whom we have contracted and to everyone whose lives we have, one way or another, willed into existence; but not to others.

Daring to Take the Lives of Enemies
Destroying enemy lives is justified if not doing so will destroy the humanistic welfare of people to whom we owe duties.

Investing in Nations
Humanistically, we owe to less developed nations investments in humanistic environments for their members, contingent on their subscribing to humanistic values.

Summary

Bibliography   155

Preface

I can suggest the aim and the general theme of this book by locating it in a few recent literary and political contexts.

The first is provided by Tony Kushner. At the beginning of the second part of *Angels in America*, the part titled *Perestroika*, the world's oldest living Bolshevik is declaiming in the Hall of Deputies of the Kremlin. He is 'unimaginably old and totally blind'. He is so old Kushner gives him the name of Aleksii Antediluvianovich Prelapsarianov. He is lamenting the collapse of Marxist collectivistic theory as a guide to the changes that are necessary in human society. Just as he declaims that we must change but that we dare not do so without some guiding 'Theory', an Angel in America crashes through the ceiling of Prior Walter's bedroom, and announces that Prior is to be the Messenger of a New Theory for our present age of anomie, of normlessness.

It seems, we later learn from the Angel, that human beings have so bankrupted the moral universe that even God has thrown up His hands in despair and abandoned everything, including His Managing Angels. They have decided that the only way to get Him back is to halt the mad human accelerated rate of normless change, and return to a condition of stasis.

The play is a dramatic and funny statement of a deep problem.

Experience versus Understanding

The second context is provided in an observation by John le Carré in an OP-ED piece in *The New York Times* of 14 December 1994. 'It is already clear to a hedgehog, as the Russians would say, that the Western powers never had the faintest idea what to do with the world if they ever freed it from Communism.'

A third context: close to the end of his gripping, almost mythic, novel, *The Waterworks*, E L Doctorow has his narrator wonder about the possible utility of writing the story which, in fact, turns out to be the novel. Writing it would, he says, be a 'ritual by which we could acknowledge ourselves for what we were. I'll grant you, perhaps it is sentimentalism to think a society is capable of being spiritually chastened in some self-educative way, of pulling itself up just one rung at a time toward moral enlightenment.'[1] Perhaps it is; but certainly *not* to think a society is so capable is to guarantee that it will not pull itself up at all.

I do not want to help guarantee that; so I make the effort that is the argument of this book.

Finally, in a penetrating essay in the March 27, 1997, *New York Review of Books*, Robert Darnton reviews and rejects several postmodern 'indictments' of the Enlightenment movement of the early eighteenth century. The now-familiar indictments are that the Enlightenment was a cover for Western cultural imperialistic destruction of other cultures; its glorification of reason undermined morality and paved the way for fascism and irrationality; and it perpetuated a macho indifference to ecological concerns and to women's rights. I think this book clarifies all those issues and shows how reason, properly understood, transcends the polemics that currently obfuscate them.

---

[1] E L Doctorow, *The Waterworks*, (New York, Random House 1994), page 236.

Part 1
Actions and Consequences

1

The Interpretation of Experience

Experience Is Not a Good Teacher
I start with the folklore that people learn from experience, and that experience is the best teacher. There is some truth to it; but without important qualification it can be dangerously inadequate and misleading.

Consider the experiences of sunrises, sunsets, and the alternation of seasons. The sensory perceptions of where the sun appears in the sky, of night and day, of warm and hot summers and cool-to-cold winters are one thing. The experience of comprehending them as effects of the rotation of the earth on its axis and the earth's angle of inclination is another thing. The sensory experiences are far from the best teachers of the understandings. Indeed, no one would learn much at all from those experiences alone.

Consider some other examples. Is the experience of a caress of a clitoris or a penis a lewd gesture, a joy of loving, a lascivious indulgence, an incestuous advance, a sharing of intimacy, natural fun? The experience itself will not teach you.

Or picture a couple of dozen men standing around in a large field. Suppose you are asked to predict their behaviour. To facilitate your prediction, you may experience them as concretely as you like. You may gaze at them, feel them, smell

Experience versus Understanding

them, listen to their voices. You may even call for any concrete information you want concerning their physiologies, anatomies, blood type, family structures, IQs, scores on personality tests, incomes, marital status, ideologies, religion, race, or ethnicity. None of it will help you in the least.

Now I give you one piece of information. They are two baseball teams (with some subs and managers) getting ready to play.

You can now predict and make sense of the behaviour of every one of them for the next couple of hours, in great detail, disregarding any of the variables noted just now. All you need is the name, 'baseball'. You can do it every time with that information; and you can never do it without it.

The reason is that you know the cultural script the name summarizes. The script tells each person what he is supposed to do in response to every other person's action; what the point of the game is; how you keep score; how long you play; what winning and losing means; what is excellent and what is lousy performance; what cheating is; how to guard against cheating; and on and on.

So it is also with respect to those two women pushing those funny little pieces of ivory around. No amount of physics or chemistry, let alone sensory experiences will teach you what they are doing; but the information that they are playing chess will tell you all about it. And so it is also with respect to whether those caresses are expression of intimacy or signals of rape. You have to bring the definitions to the experiences; you cannot learn them from the experiences.

Many of these phenomena were neatly summarized in Walter Lippmann's aphorism that first we look (the 'experiencing' step), then we name (the 'cultural' step), and only then do we see (the 'knowing' step). Were it otherwise, you would understand the marks on this page without learning to read English. (And notice the corollary: now that you have learned to read English, it is virtually impossible for you to perceive these marks as if you had not been so culturally conditioned. You cannot not understand the marks as you were taught to understand them, never mind any 'pure experiencing'.

The Interpretation of Experience

Once you have been carefully taught how and what to 'see', you cannot even get back to the pure experience, as such. The psychologist Jean Piaget captured the matter in another arresting phrase. Understanding an experience, he said, requires precisely a 'decentering' of thought from immediate sensations – as in 'knowing better' than what your senses tell you about the earth's flatness or the sun's rotation around it.

The Need for Interpretation – and Testing
Piaget's point applies not only to experiences of sensations, but equally to experiences of thoughts and emotions. We experience fear, hope, love, joy, disappointment, anger, and other emotions; and we experience baseball, jobs, family, politics, taxes, and all the mass media accounts and commentaries on all those things. Those experiences are a giant cultural step beyond the physical sensation of sunrises; but they are like that experience in one fateful respect: they too need interpretation, if we are to understand them; and we must bring the interpretation to them in the form of prior ideas, schemas, theories, or worldviews.

The question, 'How should we interpret taxes (or poverty or politics or unemployment or arguments about such things)?' is as real and important and humanly necessary as the question, 'How should we interpret sunrises and sunsets?' In some ways it is also more difficult because it calls on us to think about our thoughts, rather than just about external physical phenomena.

The problem is a little like the problem illustrated in the story of how Eve went about naming all those animals in the Garden of Eden. According to one version, she said, 'Well, it was easy, really. I called this one a rabbit, because it looks like a rabbit; and that one a lion because it looks like a lion, and so on.' That will hardly do.

On the purely cognitive intellectual level, as applied to external phenomena, we have learned to use the script of science to overcome the limitations of empirical experience. We do not always follow the rigorous script of a scientist in a

Experience versus Understanding

laboratory or observatory, of course; but we have at least learned in most cases not to assume we already know for sure just because Someone ('The Holy One,' or 'The Book', or 'Tradition') has told us so. We have learned to be puzzled, and to wonder about things. Secondly, we have learned the next essential rule of science; namely, to allow our (and everyone else's) imaginations to develop freely various guesses, conjectures, speculations ('theories' or 'hypotheses') about what something 'really is', or how something happened, or what the consequences of something might be.

And thirdly, we have learned the really distinguishing rule of science: never trust your (or anyone else's) speculations. Test them, by the severe tests of the principles of logic and then controlled empirical observation of all the logical implications.

That is how we (rationally) go about trying to solve crimes, or conduct legal trials, or plan a picnic or an advertising campaign.

Similarly, on the purely technological level, as distinct from the scientific, we have learned to use the script of pragmatism rather than magic. The test of the correctness of some technique is, 'Try it and see if it works.' If it doesn't work, go back to the drawing board and try something else. We do not usually say, if it doesn't work we must have performed the ritual wrongly, and then go on using the same methods anyway. And we have learned, more or less systematically, to think not only about the effectiveness of operations, but also about their efficiency. Not only how effectively they do the job, but how much it costs to do that job in that way with those resources, instead of using the resources for some other valued job or in some other way.

In the areas of science and technology, in short, we humans have come a long way towards realizing that we cannot trust our immediate experiences, intuitions, or tradition. Precisely by emancipating our thoughts from our direct experiences, we have learned many things that direct experiences could not possibly teach us: for example, that people's biological features are programmed by special chemicals (DNA) passed on

The Interpretation of Experience

equally by ova and sperms; that you have to be taught carefully to hate certain other people and to like modern art and music; that separate species of animals and apples have not always been there and may well not always be there; that most Americans speak English rather than Chinese for reasons of operant conditioning (which is merely a special application of the principle of evolution);[1] and so on.

What we have to learn is that we must decentre our thoughts from all our experiences in order to understand them; but that then we must judge our thoughts and our practices in terms of their consequences, not in terms of their sacred or traditional or intuitive 'rightness'. We must make them correctable by experiencing their consequences; but that is different from learning them directly through experience.

Most of us, however, continue to act in many areas as if we did not know either of those things – that we create meanings, and that we must evaluate them by their consequences. As employees, employers, voters, business people, hirers, landlords, racists (of whatever race), poor people, rich people, husbands, wives – as any such concrete role players, most people feel sure that their personal experiences and perceptions are the reliable bases of knowledge. Their grievances are naturally justified; their understandings of the world and of the other people they deal with are of course the truth. 'I know, man; I see it every day!' they say.

And it is true; they do see it every day, just as every day they see with their own eyes the sun circling the earth. But both are illusions. The sun does not circle the earth, no matter what your eyes tell you; and your experiences with members of another race or with employers or employees do not tell you why they act as they do or how they should act, no matter how certain you feel about the matter. Indeed, in the latter case, as we have noted, all you can be sure of is that you are seeing what you have been carefully (but not necessarily accurately) taught to see. Like Eve and her rabbit-naming.

For knowledge and understanding, we need some equiva-

---

[1] This point is elaborated in Chapter 2.

Experience versus Understanding

lents of the scientist's detached imagination, and detached logical and empirical testing.

The fundamental equivalent of those aids to liberation from experience is the ability to understand yourself and your experiences as objective phenomena which are really instances of certain general principles, or 'laws'. It is the ability to recognize that you are not a camera registering what is there, independently of you; you are more like a painter or a sculptor or a novelist contributing to what is there; creating your knowledge of it by adding to it your already existing speculations, theories, hypotheses, imaginings, preferences and prejudices.

When Michelangelo said that all he did as a sculptor was to liberate the Moses that had been locked in the block of marble all along, we understand that he was speaking lovely poetry. In truth, he chiselled and chiselled and polished and polished with enormous technological dexterity to turn the marble into something he had had in his imagination from the beginning. And that is the only place it was – in his mind. The sculpture of Moses is a result of what was in Michelangelo's head, plus the skill with his hands he had previously learned; it is not a result of any raw experience with the marble.

So it is also with your knowledge of your self, anyone else, a baseball game, or any other experience. Your knowledge of it is a result of what you bring to it. So far as your behavioural, emotional, and other reactions to it are concerned, it is what you define it to be. (It is not that, to me, note very importantly. To me, it is what *I* define it to be.)

Realizing that central fact of human life is the first essential requirement for liberating your knowledge from your experience. You have to get it straight from the outset and keep it in mind: your (and my and their) experiences mean nothing in or by themselves. You supply their meaning to you.

Understanding that fact is a tremendously important first step in knowing yourself, others, and society.

And an even more important conclusion follows at once; namely, that constructing the meaning of experience is the fundamental human task. Everything else follows from it – all human actions, emotions, war, peace, technology, science, justice, art, making and raising children. Everything.

Constructing the meaning is the task. Creating it. Declaring it. Deciding it.

Knowledge, Choice and Responsibility
I am entitled to say that so flatly – so seemingly dogmatically – for a deeply important reason, which makes it not dogmatic at all. The reason is the intrinsic nature of human responsibility. Note carefully:

When you act in a certain way, there are consequences of your action. If you had acted in a different way, the consequences would have been different. In that definitional sense, then, you are always in fact responsible for the consequences of your actions. If you could have acted otherwise (if it had been in you power to act otherwise), and if you knew the alternative consequences, then we can say additionally that the consequences that followed from your action are consequences for which you are also morally responsible.

That is all responsibility, and moral responsibility, as I intend the terms, mean. You are responsible for outcomes you could have made otherwise, because if you had not acted as you did, they would have been otherwise; and you are morally responsible if you knew it. It follows that once you understand that your very understanding depends on your definitions of experience, you become actually and morally responsible for choosing what definitions will govern you. Because which ones you choose will then control your perceptions of and your reactions to your experiences; and since you might have chosen otherwise, you are responsible for the choice you made, and all the consequences that flow from it.

A key phrase in the foregoing argument is, 'if it had been in your power to act otherwise.' One obvious requirement for something to be in your power to do is for you to know about it; and if you are to choose among alternatives with your eyes open, you must also know what the different consequences are likely to be of the different choices.

If you know about alternative definitions, and if you know

Experience versus Understanding

about their different consequences, you can no longer say that you should not be held responsible for the consequences of the definition you choose.

In the rest of this work I am going to try to lay out the alternative definitions available to us, and to identify their different major consequences. I will also try to persuade readers to choose one of the alternatives over the others; but that is distinct from describing them. Whether I succeed or fail in that, I hope at least to succeed in eliminating any innocence about responsibility for the consequences of choices.

Two Metaphors: the Titanic *and* Smallpox

Sometimes the image of debates about how to arrange the deck chairs on the *Titanic* is offered as a metaphor for people's preoccupation with trivia while their world is headed for disaster. Nero fiddling while Rome burned is a similar captivating image. Both, however, fail to arrest attention on the real danger of life in complex human societies. After all, there is nothing inherently wrong or inefficient about a specialization of labour or time between interior decoration and navigation, or between music and fire-fighting.

The real danger needs a different metaphor, something like having debates about whether baking soda or vinegar is the better treatment for smallpox blisters. That at least captures the perils of not sufficiently detaching thoughts from immediate perceptions to focus on the question of what causes smallpox.

The metaphor probably comes to mind because as I write, the media are carrying news of the coming political campaigns of 1996, and the aftermath of the Republican Party's 1994 capture of control of Congress. The arguments are almost entirely on the level of baking soda versus vinegar. They are about whether taxes are too high, welfare is too costly, there is too much government, congressional terms of office are too unlimited, and similar myopic preoccupations.

What should they be about? What would they be about in a society in which thoughts were more appropriately detached from concrete experiences, while remaining corrigible through

The Interpretation of Experience

feedback from their consequences? That is the question this book is about. A propositional summary of its answer is provided towards the end of Chapter 9. You might want to look at it now; but it will make more sense if you read the argument that builds up to it.

Summary: The Theses of Chapter 1

Experience Is Not a Good Teacher

The Need for Interpretation – and Testing
All experiences, from sunrises to crime taxes, require cultural interpretation; and the interpretations require testing

Knowledge, Choice, and Responsibility
If you have knowledge of alternatives and their consequences, you are responsible for the consequences of your choices.

Two Metaphors: the Titanic *and Smallpox*
Great danger lies in not thinking beyond immediate perceptions.

2

The First Choice: Deciding What It Is All For

We are going to be considering the different consequences of different definitions, and the necessity of choosing among them. At once, we come face to face with the second iron law of human existence. It is that choosing among alternatives entails evaluating their consequences; and we cannot evaluate anything unless we have a prior conception of its purpose. Its purpose is the set of consequences we want to bring into existence.

Evaluation and Purpose
You cannot tell how good a knife is unless you know what a knife is for. Suppose you decide it is for cutting things. Now you can evaluate it in terms of how well it achieves your purpose; that is, produces the consequences you want it to produce. You judge it by how well it cuts – how sharp it is; how well it holds an edge, and similar qualities that make it good for what it is for. If you are going to make a knife, you now know what qualities to give it, whereas you obviously could not do that without having a purpose for it in mind.

It is the same with everything. Coming directly to our immediate concern, you cannot know what meaning to give to experiences (including the experience of yourself and everyone else) unless you know what they are for. You can no more

Experience versus Understanding

evaluate actions or persons without knowing what they are for than you can evaluate knives without knowing what they are for.

What Are People For?
What are people and their actions for? You cannot 'find' an answer anywhere. You cannot stare at a knife ('experience' it) and learn what it is for. You have to *decide* that. Declare it. And then *bring* your definition *to* the experience of it. Otherwise it is meaningless, purposeless, pointless.

What are the alternative declarations of what people are for?

Surprisingly, perhaps, there are not many general alternatives. The most basic dichotomy is between the answer that they are for themselves, on the one hand; and that they are for something else – something 'beyond themselves', on the other. The first answer, the belief system of 'selfish individualism', says that individuals are ends in themselves and should therefore evaluate everything (their own actions, institutions, other people, belief systems, government policies...) in terms of what and how well it contributes to their personal welfare.

If they have some cultural definition of what their own welfare is, then this is an unambiguous criterion of evaluation; and life can go on in a meaningful way. We will consider the consequences of this solution a little later. Here we should simply note that for many people this conception of what people are for is so deeply ingrained that the very question, 'What are people for?' strikes them as bizarre if not shocking. 'What do you mean, "what are people for?" They are not "for" anything, they are just ends in themselves!'

The second general answer – that people are not ends in themselves, but are 'for' something beyond themselves – needs, obviously, a further specification of what the 'something' is, for which people are the means. There turn out to be three major specifications that have emerged in cultural evolution: firstly, individuals are really for other concrete individuals (the 'altruistic' answer, that you should sacrifice yourself for the welfare of other individuals); secondly, that they are for

The First Choice: Deciding What It Is All For

some more general, but still partial, collectivity of individuals, such as a nation-state, a tribe, a political party, or religion and, lastly, that they are for the most inclusive entity of all, the human species, as such.

Another way of understanding the four kinds of 'purpose' is to note that the first three declare the purpose of life to be certain *sub*systems, or parts, of the most inclusive system, the species: either the acting individuals themselves, or the other individuals with whom they identify, or a collectivity such as 'Mother Russia', or 'my country', or 'Islam' or 'Christianity'.

With any of those decisions about what life is for, you at least have the necessary basis for understanding the significance of any experience. Its significance lies in its implications for your personal welfare ('What's in it for me?'); or for the welfare of people you love ('What's in it for my family or those other people I love?'); or for your patriotic concerns ('What does it mean for America?'); or for humanity ('How does it further the human race?'). In one sense of 'meaning', any one of those conceptions of purpose at least orients you towards trying to understand the *meaning* of experiences: what does this mean for...? (Insert your own definition of purpose.)

Any of them will perform that essential function,[1] and (to repeat for emphasis) experience is meaningless without at least one of them. But it makes a big difference *which* one governs your conception of meaning, because they have very different consequences.

The Limits on the Parts of the Whole
And that brings us to the third great empirical fact about human (or for that matter, any other) existence, which limits

---

[1] The startling exception to this statement is the conception of altruism. Although traditionally thought of as the most 'elevated' and 'noble' of the sentiments, it is in fact the least viable of any of the logical possibilities. Its fatal flaw is classically illustrated in O Henry's short story, 'The Gift of the Magi'. Where altruism has been clearly important and viable in human history is in the relations of parents to their children; but what makes it viable there is precisely the a-symmetry of the relationship: the children are the dependent receivers of the altruism; but the goal of the parents and the children both is (when the system works well) for the children to become independent and 'stand on their own feet'.

Experience versus Understanding

human action as rigorously as any law of physics. It is that when entities are interdependent, the successful pursuit of the separate welfare of any *one* of them reduces the welfare of all of them.[2] That is a limit whether the interdependent entities are the organs of an organism, the members of a society, the States of the United States, or the nations of the United Nations.

The swiftest way to make the general principle vivid is to think of its operation at the level of an organism: if any cells of your body succeed in multiplying for their own sake, at the expense of other cells (or if they stop doing what other cells depend on them to do), you are in trouble. (*You,* the inclusive system, are in trouble; and therefore all the other subsystems of you are in trouble too.) Cells and organs must be so governed that they always do and only do what their inclusive system needs them to do.

The effort to analogize societies and organisms has, of course, a long and infamous history. (Governments as brains; roads as arteries; etc, etc.) What I am saying is very different. It is simply that, just as nations and organisms are equally bound by the law of gravity, they are equally bound by the law that systems are better off to the degree that their subsystems do not succeed in furthering their subsystem welfare at the expense of the system.

That is why the three conceptions of human purpose that define subsystems as what people are for (selfish individualism, altruistic individualism, or nationalisms and their kindred) are very risky for the long-term welfare of humanity. In the same way, conceptions that define the subsystems of a nation state as what people are for (for example, the separate states or regions, or corporations, or racial groups) are very risky for the long-term welfare of the nation state. To hammer the point one more time, try to imagine a symphony orchestra, each of whose members during a performance is pursuing his or her own independent ideas about her or his welfare, instead of being for the orchestra as a

---

[2] A key word in this statement is 'successful' pursuit. I will explain its importance shortly.

The First Choice: Deciding What It Is All For

whole.³ (A good approximation of the outcome is the cacophony of the tuning up process before the performance begins.)

To the degree, then, that human beings or any of their subsystem collectivities, such as nations, are interdependent, to that degree, the governing conception of what they are for needs to be the species as a whole, in its indefinite extension into the future. Since that degree is rapidly approaching its maximum (all peoples everywhere on the planet are becoming hopelessly interdependent) the luxury of selfish individualism or of selfish nationalism which may once have been tolerable becomes increasingly unaffordable.

This is no longer a romantic or utopian ideal of One World, or of universal Brotherly Love. It is simply but starkly the inexorable law that the more tightly coupled are the units of a system, the more disastrous it is for the system if units successfully pursue their unit welfare at the expense of the system.

The importance of the word, 'successfully', in that sentence now requires elaboration. It is not necessary that individuals go around consciously and 'self-sacrificingly' basing their behaviour on noble sentiments of What Is Good for Humanity. It is, rather, necessary that they live under cultural rules of the game which make contributions to the welfare of the whole *necessary for the realization of whatever self-interest they have*, even if they themselves usually do not think in those terms.

It is not necessary that the members of the symphony orchestra think, as they play their instruments, 'Now how can I play so as to further the welfare of the orchestra as a whole in this symphony?' That would be absurd. What is necessary, rather (and it is absolutely necessary), is that in order to accomplish whatever he or she personally wants to accomplish (keep the job, let us say, for the simplest selfish wish), it is made necessary that everyone do as well as possible what the

---

³ At the general level of human interdependence, two well-known models of the principle make it vivid: 'Prisoners' Dilemma' and the 'Tragedy of the Commons'. Since many readers will be familiar with those models, I will reserve a description of them for the appendix to this chapter.

Experience versus Understanding

cultural script of the game (the musical score) says he or she should do.

It is the cultural rules of the games of life (music, baseball, sex, business, welding, physics, governing – *all* of them) that we must (for the welfare of the most inclusive system) design so as to govern people's actions in accordance with the needs of the species. The rules must be such that people cannot *successfully* pursue subsystem welfare *except* in manners that further the welfare of the most inclusive system.

In the case of individualistic societies, the rules designed to channel people's selfish behaviours into socially functional outcomes are, of course, the classical rules of market economies and democratic polities. We will examine them later.[4]

Does this amount to 'controlling' individuals' behaviour? Interfering with their spontaneous autonomous actualization of their own private notions of their own private welfare? Yes; unquestionably; always.

Human beings, in the first place, do not know what they are experiencing without some prior cultural definition of their actions and the consequences. That is the first place; and it was the thesis of Chapter 1. In the second place, it is strictly impossible for them (for us) to evaluate the consequences of any definition without some prior cultural definition of purpose, which we have to learn. That was the first important point of this chapter. And in the third place, if we are interdependent, then our purpose must be the welfare of our most inclusive system, which is to say that we must design the cultural controls of our behaviour so as to contribute to that end.

Our ultimate purpose must be to optimise the welfare of the species; and therefore our proximate purpose must be to arrange our experiences so that either our characters lead us to behave accordingly, or if they do not, then the institutional mazes we construct for ourselves, so to speak, lead us to do so anyway. To adapt a familiar vocabulary, to the degree that all members of the species are interdependent, the familiar

---

[4] We will find them insufficient, but the reasons must wait until Chapter 8.

The First Choice: Deciding What It Is All For

subsystem conceptions of purpose – individualism, altruism, and collectivism (usually nationalism) – must be subordinated to humanism.

Since 'altruism' is demonstrably not a viable basis of a society, and since 'nationalisms' are, from a species point of view, only aggregated forms of individualism, in the rest of this book, I will discuss chiefly the two major worldviews of individualism and humanism.

Which leads to the next two unavoidable questions:

What do we mean by 'the welfare of the human species'; and *how* do we shape characters and/or construct appropriate mazes for ourselves?[5] Those are the issues for the next chapter.

APPENDIX

The Tragedy of the Commons

Picture a large pasture on which a hundred shepherds graze their sheep. The pasture is owned in common by everyone; hence, the name. There are a hundred shepherds, each with ten sheep. Every shepherd knows that the pasture cannot support more than about a thousand sheep in its present condition and under existing methods of sheep rearing. Above that number, the sheep will exhaust the carrying capacity of the common, and all the sheep will die.

Suppose you are one of the shepherds and you are considering whether or not to add one more sheep to your herd of ten. You know that if you do, you will increase your family's welfare by ten per cent, which may well be the difference between giving your children a college education or not. (Not to mention holidays, a car, and similar elements in your family's welfare.) You know also that if you do, the extra burden on the common will be only a tenth of one per cent – probably not even noticeable.

If those are the only facts of the case, it is rational for you to add the extra sheep. And so it is for all the other herdsmen who reason in the same way. And then another sheep, and another,

---

[5] Or is that last an impossibly self-transcending operation? Let us see.

Experience versus Understanding

and so on until the common is overgrazed, and everyone is worse off.

That is the tragedy of the common: everyone acting reasonably, but in their own interests, and the actions leading remorselessly to destruction.

Consider the essential ingredients of the tragedy. There are two.

THE ADAPTIVE PROBLEM. One is an adaptive element. The herdsmen, singly and collectively, face the pasture as one of their environments. They face it as potential producers of things to it (their wastes, fertilizers, water), and as potential consumers of things from it (the grass it grows, as well as its poison ivy). They want their environment to act in certain ways and not other ways: produce certain things and not other things; accept certain things; not demand other things. Environments, however, have needs and proclivities of their own. Some egocentric notions of some people notwithstanding, people's environments were not made for the benefit of people; so the herdsmen must do one of two things, or some combination of them.

On the one hand, if they want the environment to be more accommodating (support more sheep, for example), they must act in whatever ways are necessary to enable and empower it to do so. They must provide more water or more fertilizer; or they must improve the drainage; or they must pen up the sheep more closely at certain times; or they must breed sheep which do less damage to the common – something.

Put more generally, the herdsmen must pay certain investment costs to make the common more productive or more absorptive, and they must pay certain maintenance costs to keep the common in the condition they want it. They must, that is to say, accommodate themselves to the demands of their environment if they are to get it to accommodate itself to their demands. That, as we will see in Chapter 6, is always the secret of power: acting in ways that get others (whether other people or pastures) to act as you want them to.

To be sure, they might not be able or willing to do that. Then

The First Choice: Deciding What It Is All For

they must accept their only other option; namely, to tailor their wants to the existing level of the environment's performance. They must either accept a lower standard of living or reduce the number of people being supported by the common.

One element in the Tragedy of the Commons is people's resistance to doing either of those two things.

THE CO-ORDINATION PROBLEM. The other ingredient is even worse. It is the fact that another part of each herdsman's environment consists of all the other herdsmen, who are potential competitors as well as potential allies. As a herdsman, your problem is to co-ordinate your action with theirs. The critical question is, who should pay how much of the investment and maintenance costs of improving the pasture's productivity; and/or who should pay how much of the alternative costs of accepting a lower standard of living?

It is to your advantage to have the other herdsmen pay all of them. That is why, in the scenario with which we began, it was rational for you to add another sheep. Maybe it is even rational for you to have five children and let each of them raise ten sheep. Why should you make your family suffer a lower standard of living by not doing so? Or why should you pay for the genetic research that might lead to less destructive sheep, when you can benefit from any good results whether you pay or not?

The trouble is that it is to the others' advantage, for the same reasons, to have you pay; and so we get the tragedy.

Prisoners' Dilemma

Our second model is called 'Prisoners' Dilemma'. There are two persons, Gretel and Sam. They are interdependent in the manner shown:

		Sam	
		A	B
Gretel	1	+5, +5	−4, +6
	2	+6, −4	−3, −3

21

Experience versus Understanding

Sam gets to choose which column they will both wind up in (Column A or B), and Gretel gets to choose which row they will wind up in (Row 1 or 2). Which of the four cells they will land in is obviously a joint outcome of their separate decisions.

And it makes a big difference to them which cell they end in. The rewards (+) or costs (−) for Gretel are the first number in each cell; those for Sam are the second number. Clearly, they will be jointly better off if she chooses Row 1 and he chooses Column A; but without very special arrangements, they can't get there. Another tragedy is in the making.

For Gretel's most rational reasoning must run as follows:

Sam will choose either Column A or Column B, and since I can't control which, I must be prepared for either. Suppose he chooses A. Then if I choose Row 1, I get 5, and if I choose Row 2, I get 6; 6 is better than 5, so my best decision would be Row 2.

But suppose he chooses Column B. Then if I choose Row 1, I lose 4, whereas if I choose Row 2, I lose only 3. Losing 3 is better than losing 4, so my best choice would again be Row 2. So no matter what Sam does, I maximize my welfare by deciding on Row 2.

Sam reasons in exactly the same intelligent manner, with the rational conclusion that his best choice is always Column B. So they wind up in the worst possible outcome, Column B and Row 2, where each loses three and the pair (think of it as the GretelSam society) loses 6. In the combination Row 1 Column A, the society would have been maximally well off; and in any other combination, it would have had a net gain of 2.

Their problem is the same as the herdsmen's: how can they control their own and one another's actions so as to prevent either one from making the individually most rational decision (choosing B2 in the one case; adding another sheep in the other)?

The moral, to repeat, is that when interdependent subsystems successfully[6] pursue their strictly subsystem interests, they injure their more inclusive system, and therefore, in the long run, themselves.

---

[6] To note again the significance of the word 'successful', consider a simple change in the rules of the Commons situation: the herdsmen change the maze within they operate by providing for a police officer to check the herd sizes; and a stiff fine is

The First Choice: Deciding What It Is All For

Summary: The Theses of Chapter 2

Evaluation and Purpose
You cannot evaluate anything without a conception of what it is for.

What Are People For?
People may be conceived as for themselves or for any of several other kinds of things.

The Limits on the Parts of a Whole
An iron law of systems constrains choices: subsystems must not further their subsystem welfare at the expense of the system.

---

levied for exceeding one's limit. The fine is larger than the benefit from adding one sheep; so now self-interest dictates *not* adding a sheep. Or the instructions to the people playing Prisoners' Dilemma are changed from, 'Maximize your own welfare', to 'Your rewards will be proportional to the size of the joint welfare'. Now the rational act is to choose Row I and Column A. See also page 135.

3

The Welfare of the Species and the Shaping of Behaviour

What can it mean for the human race, as such, to be optimally well off?

Most generally, it means the same thing as the optimum welfare of any species; namely, that it, through its temporary specimens, be as well adapted as possible to all its environments – all other species and the chemical and physical features of its world. In the case of the human species, dependent as we are on cultural definitions to govern our adaptations, it means the development and maintenance of four great subsets of culture.[1]

Cultural Requirements for Human Welfare
One is a set of rules for *understanding* our environments, for accurately comprehending their natures, origins, causes, effects. These are the cultural rules of science, that stunning cultural mutation which enables our tiny brains to understand the immensity of the universe and its still tinier elementary components.[2]

---

[1] I follow the lead of two extraordinarily under-appreciated systems theorists, Russell Ackoff and Fred Emery. See 'On Ideal-Seeking Systems', Yearbook of the Society for General Systems Research, 1972, pages 17–24.
[2] Bear in mind the caveat in note 4 of Chapter 1: science, as well as the other subsets of culture discussed here, are imperatives, given the declaration of humanism. Given other declarations, these may be scoffed at. You have to choose.

Experience versus Understanding

The second is a set of rules for *coping* with those environments. For handling them, manipulating them, causing them to behave as we want them to behave – which, of course, means causing ourselves to behave so as to accommodate to their needs and natures. These are the cultural rules of sophisticated technology, another stunning cultural mutation which enables our feeble muscles to build machines to build machines that build miracles of agriculture, transport, communications, nuclear accelerators, orbiting telescopes and the other technological miracles the species has created.

Roughly speaking, those two great subsets of human culture define and govern our experiences with the world outside ourselves. The other two define and govern our experiences with the world *of* ourselves.[3]

One of them is the set of rules governing our treatment of one another: the set of rules defining what our rights are (that is, what duties others owe us); and what our obligations to others are (that is, what their rights are). These are the stunning cultural mutation of morals, which enable us to transcend our gene-driven egocentricities by overriding them. 'The Overriders of Homo Sapiens,' is the proper name of moral principles, taking 'Homo Sapiens' in its purely biological sense, as distinguished from 'human beings', whose biologies are so overlaid with culture.

For that is precisely what morals do: they command us to do what otherwise we would rather not do (stay and face the danger rather than run away, for example); or not to do what otherwise we would rather do (kill the bastard who gets in our way, for example). There is no moral principle in any culture commanding, 'Thou shalt eat what tasteth good to thee.' The reason is that there is no need for such a command; our genes take care of the matter. But there are moral commandments in every culture telling us *not* to eat what tastes good to us or do many things that feel good to us. (And to do many things that

---

[3] The distinction is only 'roughly speaking'. We use the cultural rules of science to learn also about ourselves and others, and those of technology to cope with one another. And the institutions of both science and technology themselves are parts *of* ourselves. See Richard Rorty, *Objectivity, Relativism and Truth* (1991).

The Welfare of the Species and the Shaping of Behaviour

do not feel good at all.) The reason is that our social interdependence requires us to go counter to our biological egocentrisms.[4]

What moral principles are necessary and sufficient for the new situation confronting humanity – the new situation of *species-wide* interdependence? It is the question at the heart of this book. I am working my way towards it with all deliberate reasoning.

The fourth great subset of cultural rules governing us and defining our experiences for us is the subset concerned with beauty, or the arts. Something of its nature and its somewhat peculiar status in contemporary minds, compared with science, technology, and morals, is suggested by a classical short science fiction story by Isaac Asimov, 'Nothing for Nothing'.

A scientifically, technologically, and morally advanced extraterrestrial civilization has the practice of sending scouting expeditions through the universe, with the mission of locating potential evolutionary developments that might be of use to them, and to which they might make some contribution. One of their most binding moral principles is the principle of justice that they must never take or borrow any element from any other life form or budding culture without giving something of equal value in exchange. And contrariwise: they must never give anything without receiving something they value in exchange, for that would not only be robbery; it would be insulting and dependency-encouraging. Thus the title of the story.

A scout ship happens upon planet Earth; the crew observe the very primitive cave persons killing game with rocks and pointed spears, but being limited in their hunting by the short range of their throwing arms. The crew agree that they could augment the potential of these early hominoids by introducing into their cultural definitions the technological concept of a bow and arrow. But what valuable thing to take in exchange?

Days are spent in fruitless efforts to find or think of anything

---

[4] No other social species has morals, because their *genetic* controls do for them what our moral controls do for us – if less reliably, also less rigidly.

Experience versus Understanding

valuable those creatures had to contribute. The crew is regretfully about to leave without contributing the bow and arrow technology, when one of the scouts stumbles upon a cave with drawings on the walls. That is it! What the ETs sorely lacked, and now realized what it was they lacked, was art. Gratefully, they added that subset to their culture, left the muscle-enhancing technology of the bow and arrow; and both cultures were enriched.

What good are the arts – paintings, sculptures, fiction, theatre, music, dance, and all the 'games' people invent, from football to hopscotch and chess?

The oceans of thoughtful words devoted to that question can hardly be summarized here, but the key elements might be suggested. The pursuits of science, technology, and morality are strenuous and require patience and steady self-discipline. They inevitably produce frustrations, setbacks, impatience, fatigue, and more or less articulated wonderings of what, after all, is the point?

Human beings need to be re-inspired and re-committed often; and they need some catharsis for their anger, frustration and boredom. They need re-creation. The arts and related games meet those needs.[5]

Whether high or low, elite or mass, the first characteristic of art, of course, is that it gives pleasure. That is enough for individualists; but humanists want to know further, what are the *consequences* of the *kind* of pleasure given?

Arts or games can, obviously, give pleasure in ways that do not re-inspire people to renewed efforts in a humanistic direction. Catharsis can take the form of savagery and coarseness, and people can be inspired to fascism. So, for that matter, can satisfaction of the need for cultural guides to understanding take the form of supernatural certainties rather than science. Satisfaction of the need for guides to technological coping can take the form of compulsive bureaucratic, neurotic, or magical ritual rather than pragmatic testing. Satisfaction of

---

[5] To ask how Asimov's ETs, then, managed so well without them is like asking how the cow that jumps over the moon avoids breaking her legs when she lands again on earth.

The Welfare of the Species and the Shaping of Behaviour

the need for moral guidance can take the form of the command, do unto others what they would do unto you, only do it first, rather than the command to treat them justly.

Our point at the moment is not just that human beings need cultural definitions to interpret their experiencings (I established that, I hope, in Chapter 1); but that *if* the new situation of species-wide interdependence is to be met in the interest of the species, *then* the cultural definitions must be of a certain kind. What kind, I have been attempting to describe briefly. (Science, sophisticated technology, moral rules defining the species as 'the point', and art which inspires people to the purpose of the species.)

But none of this is to say that other kinds are not possible; it is only to say that they will lead to the Tragedy of the Commons on a planetary scale. There is nothing in nature to prevent that, except the *potential* of human nature to comprehend the facts. I am trying to nurture that potential a little.

Shaping Human Behaviour
How do we come to comprehend and therefore respond to things the way we do – whether superstitiously or scientifically, brutally or gently? How do we become the cultural sorts of persons we are, controlled by the internal controls that govern us? We need to understand those becomings if we are to get ourselves to comprehend and adjust to them humanistically and responsibly, rather than only individualistically or nationalistically.

We need to comprehend the facts of how we come to be the people we are with the comprehensions we have.

This is also a comprehension that does not come naturally to human beings, any more than comprehension of solar systems and electrons comes naturally. It too requires a certain detachment of thought from everyday senses of experience. Here above all we need to distance ourselves from ourselves in order to consider objectively how we acquire our cultural selves.

We acquire them through the same basic principles that produced our biological selves (and those of all other living

Experience versus Understanding

things): the principles of evolution. Put simply, those basic principles are that, at any given time, inside all entities (from atoms through molecules to organisms and our character structures) variations in behavioural determinants can occur, more or less by chance.[6] Some of those that occur may be better suited to various aspects of the entity's environments than others. Those better suited get reinforced, simply by definition of 'better suited'; and those worse suited do not get reinforced, or may even be extinguished. Some variations may be irrelevant to an entity's environment; and then the environment is irrelevant to the shaping of behaviour.

(Many reports of the identical behaviours of identical twins even though they were raised in very different environments are interpreted as showing that behaviour is determined only by genetic inner controls – by heredity. The behaviour in question, however, is behaviour to which the twins' environments are indifferent; the environments simply do not do any differential selecting. Where your environment doesn't care, so to speak, what you do about eating spinach, whether or not you eat spinach will be entirely a matter of your internal tastes, whether dictated by your genes or by your *previous* environments.)

When environments do 'select' some variations for perpetuation, and not others; they thereby shape the nature of the entity.

The major shaping environments of every human being at infancy consists of other people, most saliently, 'parents,' and/or other more or less nurturing persons. (We may as well refer to them all simply as shapers.) Shapers very directly and usually deliberately select for reinforcement (with rewarding responses from coos and bravos to candy treats and – later on – money and applause) *some* of the sounds, facial expressions, gestures, movements, behaviour, actions the child, and later the adult, will produce; and will not reinforce – or will punish – others.

As surely as certain primates with opposable thumbs were

[6] Some entities, we must note for later elaboration, may be programmed for internal variations. People 'programmed' by the cultural rules of science and 'technological progress' are prime examples.

The Welfare of the Species and the Shaping of Behaviour

once selected out by certain environments to become Homo sapiens, the elements of our character structures were (and are being) selected out by our environing shapers to become you and me. For better and/or for worse.

We are characterologically what got selected out of our various inner-generated ploys, wigglings, and gambits by Them – all those (more *and* less nurturing) 'others' to whose preferences our preferences were more or less suited.[7] We continue to be characterologically what continues to prove suited to our environing others (those with power, that is); or our internal controls change if changes prove better suited. (Or, of course, we fail to adapt.)[8]

Those 'others' shaped and are constantly reinforcing or reshaping (or ignoring – being indifferent to) our character-istic ways of defining our selves, our experiences, other people, and our notions of what we and they are for.

Knowledge and Responsibility
Understanding that fact is a fruit of the tree of knowledge that all who would play God should want us not to know: the knowledge that every conception we have which tells us what we are experiencing, including our very conceptions of ourselves and what we are for, *are products of our shapings*. Our characterological internal controls are *outcomes*: results, consequences, effects. They are the immediate, proximate, causes of our behaviour; but the ultimate causes are the shapings that produced them.

The reason a jealous god might not want us to have that knowledge is that it empowers us to choose what shapings to impose on ourselves and others; and makes us responsible for the consequences of whatever shapings we support.

If you know that the path you take is dictated by the structure

---

[7] And whose power was greater than ours, less than ours, or about the same – it makes a large difference. But power is a crucial variable that will have to wait a while for our full attention (see Chapter 5).

[8] One reason we may fail to adapt to environing others is that, once they are formed, our characters themselves can become the shapers of our further character development: we can reward and punish ourselves; and thus – for better or for worse – become immune to external sanctions. More on this complexity later.

Experience versus Understanding

of the maze you are in, and if you know how to construct mazes, you become responsible for the path you take. The mazes that shape human behaviour are the cultural rules that govern how people behave towards one another;[9] and how people behave towards one another is the process that shapes human character. The fact that we are products, then, does not absolve us from responsibility. Rather, it is a stunningly important seeming-paradox that knowing we are determined makes us more responsible for our actions than not knowing.

The knowledge of the fact requires us to accept the responsibility for constructing the rules of understanding, of technology, of catharsis and inspiration, and of morality that will further the welfare of the species.

Or else the responsibility for the opposite consequences. For whatever the consequences are of actions we take, they are consequences we have chosen if we know how they could have been otherwise. I think that the knowledge that this is so has more profound implications for our behaviour as human beings than any other knowledge.

Because it is so important, I will elaborate in more detail in the next chapter the determinants of our actions; and how those determinants become what they are.

Ecclesiastes
Before concentrating on those details, however, we must immunize ourselves against a too-easy misinterpretation of the idea of responsibly constructing our mazes. One of the harder parts of being humanistically human is to learn the importance of the lesson in Ecclesiastes that there is a time for everything, and not all things can be done at the same time.

There is a time for playing with all one's consciousness the game of baseball by the rules of baseball; and a very different time, after the season, to think with all one's consciousness about whether the rules should be changed so as to produce different behaviour next season. The two activities, following

---

[9] The mazes that shape the behaviour of baseball players are the (enforced) rules of baseball.

The Welfare of the Species and the Shaping of Behaviour

the script and considering how or whether to change the script, are radically different; and doing either one when the metascript calls for doing the other is crazy. It would mean doing neither.

And failing to do both, at their separate times, while not perhaps crazy is definitely not humanistic. Never examining the scripts governing one's – and one's fellows' – behaviour is remaining an ignorant slave of them. Always examining them and never playing the games they prescribe is never getting the day started. This book is mostly about the importance of examining the mazes, because not enough of that is done; but it would be a horror to think of it as a substitute for, or in competition with, all the books about all the games we play once the days start.

Summary: The Theses of Chapter 3

Cultural Requirements for Human Welfare
The long-term welfare of the human species requires effective moral rules for the pursuit of understanding, technological coping, justice, and art; and those rules require certain kinds of people.

Shaping Human Behaviour
We become the people we are through a basic principle of evolution: internal controls lead to actions which environments differentially select for survival.

Knowledge and Responsibility
Once we know the ways people are shaped, we become responsible for how people are shaped, if we have power.

4

Why We Act As We Do

I have said that our character is the set of inner controls that govern our behaviour, and that those controls are products of the rewarding and unrewarding 'selections' made by our environing others. Both parts of that statement now need elaboration and justification.

I begin with a simple case which, however simple it is, contains all the relevant elements of all actions.

The Determinants of Our Decisions
It is most efficient to formulate the issue as the question, 'What determines the likelihood that a person will act in a certain manner?' By 'a certain manner', I mean doing anything at all – taking a job, leaving a job, cheating, voting for Jones, kissing him or her, being conscientious – anything at all. Call it X. To develop the basic answer, let X be a very simple action. Let it be the action of paying ten dollars to play a certain game, the Choosing Boxes Game.

I will identify eleven variables (I will call them decision variables) which determine the likelihood that you will do that X.[1] The game is simple. You get to choose one box from among

[1] In the following discussion, I try to make accessible to everyone the work of many specialists, especially Alfred Kuhn (1974), William Powers (1973), George C Homans (1974), and Orville Brim (1956).

Experience versus Understanding

ten identical sealed boxes. The boxes themselves are worthless. You will own the contents of the box you choose. I will compare the likelihood of your deciding to pay the ten dollars (do that X) in two different circumstances: situation A and situation B.

Firstly, suppose that in Situation A you think all the boxes are empty, while in Situation B you think that at least some of them contain something valuable. You are more likely, are you not, to pay the ten dollars in Situation B than in Situation A? Let us put that greater likelihood in the form of a general rule. Other things equal, people are likely to do any X *to the degree that they think there is some possible rewarding consequence of doing it.*

Secondly, suppose that in Situation A you think the boxes contain used birthday candles from previous birthday cakes, and in Situation B that they contain large sums of money. You are more likely, are you not, to pay the ten dollars in Situation B? The general principle is: Other things being equal (a phrase I will omit from now on but always assume), people are likely to do any X *to the degree that they value greatly the possible rewarding consequences.* (In the case of each principle, by the way, the 'other things' that I assume to remain equal are simply the other ten decision variables I am in the process of identifying.)

Thirdly, suppose that in Situation A you think the boxes contain pictures of your mother, and in Situation B, pictures of your father. Suppose you have a dozen pictures of your mother and none of your father (and suppose you like(d) them both equally). You are more likely, I suggest, to pay the ten dollars in Situation B. General principle: People are likely to do any X *to the degree that they feel relatively deprived of the rewards they think might be a consequence of doing it.*

Fourthly, suppose you think that in Situation A one of the boxes contains a hundred dollars, the rest being empty; and in Situation B that *nine* of them contain a hundred dollars, the remaining one being empty. You are more likely to pay the ten dollars in Situation B. The general principle is: People are likely to do any X *to the degree that they think the probabilities are high that doing it will in fact pay off in the possible rewarding consequences.*

Fifthly, suppose that in Situation A you think any money in

Why We Act As We Do

the boxes will become yours twenty years from now, and in Situation B that it will be yours at once. You are more likely to do the X of paying ten dollars in Situation B. General principle: People are likely to do any X *to the degree that the time period they think will elapse between doing the X and getting the benefits is satisfactory.* (Notice that I have phrased this principle more cautiously than saying that they are likely to do so if they think the time period is short. The reason for the caution is that some people might prefer future rewards over present rewards.)

Sixthly, suppose that in Situation A you think some of the boxes contain an angry scorpion, no matter what goodies the others might contain, and in Situation B you think all the boxes not containing goodies are empty. You are more likely (other things being equal, remember) to pay the ten dollars in Situation B. General principle: People are likely to do any X *to the degree that they do not perceive any possible costly or undesirable consequences of doing so.*

THE MATTER OF COSTS. Here we must pause a moment on the concept of costs. In all the situations considered so far, and to be considered below, one cost is always involved; namely, the ten dollars. That is an example of one kind of cost, 'opportunity costs'. The real cost of paying the ten dollars to play the game consists of sacrificing thereby all the other things you could have done with the ten dollars. What you lose are many opportunities to get other benefits.

All actions entail opportunity costs. Doing any X means not doing a thousand other things you could have done with the time, energy, money, and any other resource that was involved in doing the X. In addition, many, but not all, actions entail another kind of cost, 'disutility costs'. They are the unpleasant things you would prefer to avoid that are inherently involved in the action, such as ants and mosquitoes at the picnic. The scorpion I introduced in the sixth little decision situation is an example. (Purists say, correctly, that this is really an opportunity cost also: you sacrifice freedom from mosquitoes, for example. It may be useful, however, to preserve a distinction between resources, for example, money, lost in choosing

Experience versus Understanding

an X, and pain incurred as an accompaniment of X.)

With costs understood, we can now return to the decision variables, the next four of which also concern costs. The seventh is this: suppose that in Situation A you think at least one of the boxes contains a scorpion as the possible costly consequence of playing the game, and in Situation B you think the possible cost is that at least one contains a worm. Assuming for the moment that you do not have a peculiarly strong hangup about worms, you are more likely to pay the ten dollars in Situation B. General principle: people are likely to do any X *to the degree that any possible cost foreseen is relatively unimportant to them.*

Eighthly, suppose that in Situation A you are down to your last ten dollars, and in Situation B you have a lot of tens in your wallet. Other things equal, you are more likely to pay the ten dollars in Situation B. The general principle is: people are likely to do any X *to the degree that they already have a lot of whatever they must forgo in doing X.* (They can easily afford it.)

Ninthly, suppose that in Situation A you think nine of the boxes contain a scorpion, and in Situation B only one of them does. You are more likely (other things being equal) to pay the ten dollars in Situation B. General principle: people are likely to do any X *to the degree that they think the probabilities are low that any possible cost will in fact have to be paid.* (You may think of 'daredevils' as people who prefer risky actions, but they are really playing a different game, such as 'Show How Brave You Are,' rather than 'Choosing Boxes'.)

Tenthly, suppose that in Situation A you think one of the boxes contains a poison gas that is instantly lethal, while in Situation B you think one of them contains a gas whose harmful effects will not appear for at least eighty years. You are more likely to pay the ten dollars in Situation B. General principle: people are likely to do any X *to the degree that the time period they think will elapse between doing it and having to pay any costs is satisfactory.*

We now have five variables that deal with various aspects of the benefits or rewards of an action and five that deal in parallel fashion with costs. But there is clearly one more variable to be entered into the picture. Suppose you perceive that you do not have ten dollars and cannot beg, borrow, or steal it. We can go right to the general principle, and don't let the obviousness of this particular case fool you: people are likely to do any X (other things being equal) *to the degree that they think they have the ability to do it.*

Those eleven variables are the immediate causes of your behaviour. Your notions of what action available to you in the circumstances will most likely bring you the most of what you value and cost you the least are what cause you to act as you do.

THE IMMEDIATE CAUSES ARE INSIDE YOU. Notice a crucial fact concerning those statements about the causes of behaviour. It is that all the immediate causes of your behaviour are in your mind. It is *your perception* of possible rewarding consequences that helps to determine the probability that you will do the act, *your perception* of possible costs, the importance *you* attach to the rewards and costs, and so on. It is not what is in the boxes; it is what you *think* is in the boxes (and how you feel about those things) that are the immediate causes.

The values of those eleven variables are at least part of what is meant by a person's 'character'. The kinds of things a person values and tries to get; the kinds she tries to avoid; his optimism or pessimism about the chances of success; her preference for short-term benefits over long-term considerations; his willingness to take risks as compared to his risk-aversion; the intensity of her desires; the level of his self-confidence – those are the qualities the decision variables specify more formally. They help to distinguish one person's character structure from another's; and in that sense, we can say that the immediate determinant of a person's actions is the person's character.

Notice also an extremely important corollary of that understanding. It is that when a person acts in a certain manner, you learn something at once about that person. You learn that her character is the sort that leads to that behaviour. A particularly important kind of behaviour with that significance is verbal behaviour. When people say things about objects, or events, or other people, what you learn is something about the speakers; not about the things or the people.

Experience versus Understanding

In a little more detail, when you tell me that you saw James act in a certain way, I can learn nothing about James's actions; I can learn, in the first instance, only one thing: that you want me to think that you think you saw James act in that way. For all I know, you may be lying, you may be deluded, you may have dreamed it, someone may have planted the thought in your mind, you may be joking. There may be many reasons for your saying that you saw or heard something, other than the possibility that you actually did.

When you use verbs and nouns, I learn *what* you want me to think you think about things and their actions. When you use adjectives, I learn *how* you want me to think you feel about things. Since the immediate causes of your behaviour are inside you, I can infer from your behaviour only what is inside you. That may give me a hypothesis about the other person or event; but I need to check that out independently.

THE CASE OF BEHAVIOUR MODIFICATION. For another little model of the immediate causes of behaviour, I will use a case in which the concept of 'character' is not relevant; but the determining variables are still the same. This is the famous – or in some views, the infamous – work of the late B F Skinner. As will become clear, this model will also serve as a transition to our concern with the question of the determinants of the immediate causes – the determinants of character, or internal controls. It will also become clear the sense in which operant conditioning is an instance of general evolutionary principles.

Skinner did much of his work with pigeons, and is famous for training the pigeons to act in diverse ways. The technique is simplicity itself, in principle. All Skinner did is to put the pigeon in an environment rigged so that there is one and only one way (one behavioural X) for the pigeon to get the reward it wants (some grain); namely, by doing what Skinner wanted it to do.

The technique is, in fact, an implicit application of the decision variables, although most behavioural psychologists do not usually present the matter in these terms. In failing to do

Why We Act As We Do

so, they often contribute to some misunderstanding of the nature of behaviour modification.

To influence the pigeon's behaviour, a behavioural psychologist first ascertains what is important to the pigeon – what will make the pigeon feel good (decision variable number two). This step nearly always goes unnoticed because everyone knows so well that pigeons value grain; not fish bones, not dollars, not words of praise, and so on. It is a crucial step, however, as you can realize by imagining that someone tried to get his pigeons to peck certain circles on its box (let us say) by offering them dollars or praise as a payoff. The result would simply be one maladapted psychologist. It is a crucial step to recognize for a second reason too. Recognizing it makes clear something that many people who are hostile to behaviour modification may overlook. That is that, if you want to influence someone's behaviour, you must start by accepting that person's nature and values. It is the pigeon's preferences, not yours or mine or the psychologist's that everyone had better accept.

The evolutionary principle is at work here as everywhere: it is our *environment* to which we must adapt.

That understood, the second step is to make sure the pigeons feel relatively deprived of the grain (our third decision variable). Psychologists do this coercively, by starving them a little. In human affairs, of course, this is one of the harder things to do, which (fortunately or unfortunately; we will see) is one of the reasons it is easier to control pigeons' behaviour than persons'.[2]

Next, the psychologist arranges things so that there definitely is a 'possible rewarding consequence' of pecking the circle (our first decision variable). She provides a payoff in grain for it; and, of course, she relies on the fact that the pigeon is already internally programmed, genetically, to peck as a way of getting the food it wants. She then further arranges the environment so that the probabilities are high that pecking the circle will in fact result in the receipt of grain (decision variable number four); and so that there is not too

---

[2] This is one of the places at which *power* becomes important. See Chapter 5.

Experience versus Understanding

long a time interval between the pecking and the reward (decision variable number five).

The five variables concerning costs are hardly ever mentioned by behavioural psychologists; they take them for granted. We, however, who are trying to understand in detail why people (or pigeons) act as they do, cannot afford to take them for granted. And, in fact, any psychologist must pay sharp attention to them implicitly, even if she does not write about the matter explicitly. What she does is to make sure that the probability is zero that the pigeon will perceive or experience any disutility costs for doing what she wants it to do; and that the pigeon is effectively satiated with all the rewards it will have to forgo as the opportunity costs entailed in pecking the circle (water, sex, sleep, etc). There are no cats lunging at the pigeon; it does not get an electric shock when it pecks the circle; the box is warm enough and dry enough; and so on.

Finally, consider the eleventh decision variable, the matter of ability. What Skinner was very careful never to do (even if he never mentioned the fact) is to try to make the pigeon sing 'The Star-spangled Banner', fly a kite, solve an equation, or ten thousand other things. Only pecking, walking, and the like: actions within the pigeon's range of abilities.

BEHAVIOUR IS DETERMINED. People's actions are determined. They are determined by the values of the decision variables inside their heads; they are determined by people's character. That is why, as we have noted, when people act, we can learn something about their characters. If we think of the values and perceptions inside people's heads as their 'free will', we can answer a famous question in an interesting and very serious way. The question is, 'Is human action determined, or is it a matter of free will?' We can now answer: it is determined by free will.

But where, then, did that free will – the internal controls, the values of the decision variables – come from? What determines the immediate causes?

Our answer is two-fold. Partly it is that people's experiences in previous situations (as the people interpreted those

Why We Act As We Do

experiences) determine them; partly it is (as Chapter 1 emphasized) that their culture tells them how to define any present situation, as well as all the previous ones.

Experiences as Determinants
Return, for a start, to the behavioural psychologist and her pigeons. Our emphasis above was on the ways in which she must, in any given situation in which she deals with a pigeon, accept the values of the pigeon's decision variables in that situation. For those will be the immediate causes of the pigeon's behaviour. Now we emphasize a second point; namely, that by her actions, the psychologist unavoidably affects the values of those variables, causing them either to change or not to change. (By the same token, as we will see, they affect her notions of what will make *her* feel well adapted.)

It works essentially as follows: up to the point of the pigeon's encounter with the experimenter, it has been getting along fine not pecking circles. It has been getting its grain, let us suppose, by pecking it out of a food tray in the laboratory. (Why did it do that? Because it valued the possible consequence of getting grain, thought pecking in the tray had a high probability of yielding the payoff, thought there were no probable costly consequences, had the ability to peck, and so on.)

Suppose the experimenter now changes the rules of the game. She puts the pigeon in a situation where there is no food tray. What to do? The pigeon usually pecks around more or less aimlessly, maybe gives a few really heavy pecks as the frustration mounts, ruffles its feathers, pecks at something else. Let us anthropomorphize freely, and suppose it begins to mutter truculently and aggressively about what a lousy, unreasonable, unloving, and unfair bastard that psychologist really is.

No matter. Sooner or later, if the psychologist doesn't panic, the pigeon will peck the circle. (Or, if we continue to anthropomorphize, it will finally listen to advice about the new rules, and its own new role, and instantly peck the circle.)

Instant reward: grain. Sooner or later it hits the circle again. More grain. Again: more grain. Maybe it tries the tray again – *no grain.*

Experience versus Understanding

The pigeon learns a new perception: in this sort of situation, the probabilities are high $(1.0)^3$ that pecking a circle will result in grain and in no costs, and the probabilities are low (0.0) that any other X will have the same result. The pigeon is converted; it becomes a dedicated circle pecker.

There is, in fact, no way in which that pigeon can avoid becoming a confirmed circle pecker, if it lives, and if the psychologist does not change her behaviour.[4] From now on, it will act differently, because the values of its decision variables are different. They are different because the different environment to which it had to adapt was one which did not respond to the old values; it responded only to the new ones. So now a different set of values of the same decision variables are the immediate determinants of the pigeon's actions.

Why does the pigeon act the way it does? Because the values of its decision variables are what they are; because that is the way it thinks will most likely make it feel good. Why does it think that? Because those are the values of the decision variables that paid off in the environment to which the pigeon had to adapt.

Why do you get in your car or on a subway or bus in order to get from here to there, instead of hitching your horse up to your carriage and saying, 'Giddyup'? Because in the environment to which you have learned to adapt, you do not have the resources for doing that second X (and if you just stood around saying, 'Giddyup, Giddyup,' it wouldn't get you far in a direction you would like), whereas that first X works

---

[3] An important modification of the simplified procedure I have sketched is to give the reward only *randomly* in response to the pecking. This makes pecking (for example) a necessary but not a sufficient condition for the reward. It has the effect of taking longer to educate the learner; but once the learning has occurred, future disappointments are less likely to extinguish the behaviour. ('All I know is that the pecking is necessary. No one promised me a rose garden.')

[4] It is at this point that the big difference between human beings and other creatures that I have been emphasizing becomes crucial. Human beings may *interpret* the change in the situation in many different ways which prevent them from changing their behaviour, even if death is the outcome. They may define the change as a test of their fidelity to the old norms; as a test of their faith in God (cf. Abraham and Job); as an opportunity heroically to defy the Nazi psychologist; and on and on. Sometimes people do not change.

well. And so, if you will just stop to think about it, it is with all the other Xs you do.

Why do some people act differently from other people? For the same kinds of reasons some pigeons peck round dots and others do not: what they had learned was the most beneficial and least costly behaviour in their earlier experiences was different. From people's behaviour, then, we can learn not only about the nature of their present characters, but also something about the nature of their earlier environments. As we will see, the knowledge that this is so has profound implications for our moral responsibilities towards other people.

PREFERENCES AND ABILITIES. What about the pigeon's preference for grain, and the ability to peck. Where did they come from?

In the pigeon's case, of course, they came from the *genetic* programmes that *bio-chemically* govern the pigeon's development. That is where our preferences for oxygen and for bladder-emptying came from also, along with a few other preferences and some basic abilities. For far and away the most part, however, your preferences and your notions of which Xs will have what consequences with what probability in what time period – those values of your decision variables came from the *cultural* programmes that *socio-psychologically* governed your development.

Culture as Determinant

BASEBALL AS EXAMPLE. To make this clear, think again about the game of baseball. Why do baseball players value hits and runs (for their team), and try to avoid errors and outs? Why do they always (*always*) run to the right of home plate when they get a hit, and *never* to the left? Why do they count and compare runs so assiduously? Why don't they tackle runners?

Because, of course, the cultural rules of the game of baseball tell them exactly what the value of every decision variable is from moment to moment; and their past experiences have taught them those rules.

Experience versus Understanding

The script of baseball tells every player what he must do, must not do, and may do at every moment – the 'mays' usually referring to various tactics and strategies for winning. The script of baseball further tells everyone what the point of the game is. It defines 'winning' and 'losing', 'succeeding' and 'failing'. It defines preferences within the game: goals, purposes, aims.

It is important to let the magnitude of this fact register fully in your mind. Cultural scripts create the point of activities. It is the script and only the script that makes any sense of winning/losing, succeeding/failing. The script additionally says what is excellent and what is poor role performance. It, and only it, tells you how to keep score for the teams and how to measure role performance. *It tells you what to want and how to evaluate.*

Finally, the game as scripted necessarily entails opportunities for people to cheat (for example, do the must-nots, such as spitting on the ball); it generates motives to cheat ('Win!' and 'Perform Brilliantly!'); and it involves various devices to prevent cheating (umpires, for example, and rules about fines, suspensions, being thrown out of games, and the like).

The script of baseball defines for baseball players that fundamentally important factor of human 'feeling good', self-respect and mattering. It tells you that playing or watching baseball is a way of getting self-respect (it is one of the things that 'real men' do, and women also to a lesser degree in American society); and it tells you exactly what you must do in playing baseball, or being a fan of baseball, to feel self-respect.

GENERALIZING BASEBALL. My purpose, to repeat, in reviewing all those features of baseball in those general terms is to elaborate and specify the point that the terms I have used apply to nearly all human activities. Certainly, the activities with which we will be concerned in this book are all culturally scripted, with the scripts specifying the following matters:

Why We Act As We Do

1 What the statuses and roles are in which the activities are carried out.
2 How they are organized into what organizations, if they are.
3 What the point of the activity is; that is, the meaning of succeeding/winning, failing/losing.
4 How you keep score (how you *measure* success).
5 When to begin and end.
6 What sorts of people should be recruited to the different roles, how they should be motivated, and how they may be got rid of.
7 What the standards of excellent role performance are, and how you measure performance.
8 What cheating is.
9 How to prevent or minimize cheating.

Those prescriptions, rules, and definitions are the internal controls human beings learn from one another through parental do's and don'ts and modellings; and in modern societies through the even more potent do's and don'ts and modellings of peers, movies, novels, television, advertisements, and other teachers of many different kinds and substances. It is a hallmark of modern societies that there are *many different* scripts for sex, marriage, family behaviour, masculinity, femininity, work, leisure, politics, religion – every possible area of human life. That radically complicates not only the task of understanding just which internal controls are controlling a given person's actions at a given time, but also the task of integrating the behaviour of variously controlled persons into a viably coherent society. It does not, however, alter the fundamental principle that each set of cultural scripts specifies for the persons it controls the nine matters identified above.

Cultural Games as Mazes
An important analogy should be apparent. In fact, it is more than an analogy. The cultural rules of the activities in which people engage are precisely homologous to the structure of an

Experience versus Understanding

environment in which a behavioural psychologist gets a pigeon to act in a certain way. The rules are even homologous to the genetic structure of the pigeon which causes it to want grain and not want, say, electric shocks. The 'experiences' from which people learn are the culturally prescribed responses of *their* environments to their actions, however different those environments may be, one from another.

Given that the pigeon wants grain, and given that its environing psychologist has arranged things so that the probability is 1.0 that pecking a circle will elicit the grain and 0.0 that any other action will do so, and given that the pigeon is able to peck, the probability is very high that the action the pigeon will display is circle-pecking. Given a different environing psychologist with a different governing idea about desirable pecking, the probability is just as high that *her* pigeon will *not* be a circle pecker.

Cultural game rules tell individuals what to value (for example, what desirable behaviour for a baseball pitcher consists of); and they arrange things so that certain behaviour has certain probabilities of eliciting valued responses from other people, and other behaviour has lower or zero probabilities of doing so. They even provide (or they prescribe whether or not to provide) the abilities to conform to the rules. Given the rules of baseball, the probability is very high that the action a pitcher will display is throwing a baseball, and very very low that he will throw a football or do thirty-seven thousand other things you and I could easily think of.

If you know the cultural rules specifying the nine elements noted above in any situation (the actually operating, governing rules, of course; not just what someone says the rules are or 'should be', or wishes they were); then you know the values of players' decision variables; and you know how and why the persons involved will act.

Scripts, Decisions and Actions
The immediate reason the values of people's decision variables are what they are is that that is the way the scripts of the games they are playing tell them they should be in order to win –

Why We Act As We Do

however 'win' is defined in those particular games. Cultural scripts may require Christians to persecute Jews in unspeakable ways (Isban Deak, 1989) and to risk torture to help Jews escape persecution (Philip Hallie, 1979.) They may require white teenagers to beat up and kill blacks; black boys to gang-rape white women; white American soldiers to gang-rape Vietnamese girls; Mother Theresa to devote her life to almost hopeless Indian cases of leprosy; millions of people to lead lives of quiet desperation or contented placidity.

Any concrete action that is physically possible may be ordered or forbidden for the sake of power and self-respect; and people will act in any of the ways that led Sartre to conclude that 'Hell is other people'; or any of the more pleasant ways that can just as easily make us think heaven is other people. It all depends on which ways seem most likely to enhance self-respect; to give people the feeling that they are behaving desirably. It depends on what sort of mazes they were made or permitted to find their way around in. And the mazes human actors find their way around in are the scripted responses of their environing others to the behaviours the *actors'* currently controlling scripts have elicited from them.

In the following chapters, I elaborate on the four sentences in the preceding paragraph. The principle that should at this point be clear is that we ought to be very thoughtful about the scripts we allow to be so controlling.

Summary: The Theses of Chapter 4

The Determinants of Our Decisions
The immediate determinants of our behaviour are the values of eleven variables inside us, often referred to as 'character' or 'free will'.

Experiences as Determinants
The major determinants of those internal controls are experiences prescribed and interpreted by culture.

Experience versus Understanding

Culture as Determinant
All human activities are governed by cultural rules stating the nine critical elements specified by the rules of baseball.

Cultural Games as Mazes
Consequently, the institutional games of life are homologous to the mazes causing laboratory animals to run the paths they run.

Scripts, Decisions and Actions
The immediate reason the values of our decision variable are what they are is that that is what the cultural scripts governing us say they should be.

5

Power, Behaviour, and Success

So far we have been focusing only on the 'you' consisting of your decision variables: your likes and dislikes, conceptions of rewards and costs, time preferences, notions about what works and doesn't work, conceptions of how others are likely to react, and so on. In short, your values and your understandings. We have been focusing on your character or, if you like, on you as manifested in your free will. We have been focusing on what makes you tick: on the internal controls of your behaviour, and on some of their determinants.

We now turn to another of their determinants, and (more closely related than is commonly thought) to the determinants of your success in life: your power.

The Nature of Power
By 'power,' I mean simply the probability that you will succeed in getting the people in your environment to act as you want them to act.

That is the main determinant of your welfare as you define your welfare: how able you are to get other people to give you what you want (money or praise, say); accept from you what you want them to accept (your labour skills or artwork, say); leave alone what you don't want them to take (your secrets or your wallet); and not inflict on you

Experience versus Understanding

anything you do not want (hazardous wastes, or insults).

Unlike the immediate determinants of your actions (namely, the values of your decision variables), the determinants of your power are definitely *not* inside you. Your power is determined by five things: how much other people value what you have to offer them (your looks, skills, money, pole-vaulting prowess, vote, approval, knowledge, love, or whatever, very much including your potential for frustrating them); how many such people there are; how many competitors you have making the same offers (or threats) to them; how willing and able the others are to act as you want them to act (you can't get blood from a stone); and how willing and able you are actually to make your potential offerings available to them. This last, in turn, is related to how badly you want or need their conformity to your expectations.

Put in slightly different terms, other people are likely to act as you want them to act (you have power) to the degree that five things are true:

1 What you offer them as inducement is something they greatly need or want.
2 There are many of them out there eager for your offering. (They have a lot of competition to please you; and they know it.)
3 There are not many like you, making that offer.
4 The way you want them to act is within their abilities and isn't too costly for them.
5 You are willing and able actually to carry through on your offer. (You are ready to do what they require in exchange for their conformity.

The values of those variables determine your power. What determines *them*?

Game Scripts and Power
We have established, I trust, that the values of people's decision variables are given, directly or indirectly, by the cultural scripts

of the games in which they are caught up. The scripts of the game-like activities of schooling, dating, baseball, science, or whatever, prescribe what is rewarding, what costs are, what you have to do to win the benefits, what the odds are, and so on.

It is the same when we seek the determinants of the values of the power variables: we must look at the cultural rules of the games people play.

What specific offerings are valued by others depends on whether you are playing tennis, computer programming, hard rock, motherhood, or something else. Whether a woman's small feet, ankles, thighs, breasts, or buttocks are or are not power bases in sexual games depends not on biology but on prevailing cultural dictates of what is erotic. How many people are demanding various offerings as consumers, and how many are offering them as producers, are affected by rules concerning discrimination, opportunities to acquire skills, notions about appropriate girls' tastes and boys' tastes and 'in' tastes, and similar cultural scripts. How badly you should want various things, and how willing you should be to do various things are also culturally scripted to a great degree. When and about what to be gung-ho, laid back, or repelled is a matter of game rules and styles. Whether individual offerings may include land, factories, oil wells, and the like (that is, whether the rules are those of capitalism or not) is an historically dramatic determinant of power.

A striking fact to notice about your power is that the things that determine that vital aspect of you are not within your power to control. In fact, they are more characteristic of the other people in your environment than of you. Your power is determined by how much other people value your offerings; how many of them there are; how many other people are competing with you; how able and willing the others are to comply with your wants.

Notice an important implication of this last point. The implication becomes at once clear if we simply restate the point: one of the reasons you may be powerless to get what you want from others is that they do not have enough power. Their

Experience versus Understanding

power, of course, is determined by the same variables as yours. Two of them are the intensity of their desires for your offerings and their willingness and ability to act as you want them to act – pay you, for example. In their relations with you, their power and your power are less if they do not have, and you cannot or will not give them, greater incentives and abilities to do what you want.

One of the things that can go wrong for you – mark the point – is that other people do not have enough power. For a simple but important example, the reason a shop assistant in New York has a higher level of living than an equally skilful and industrious shop assistant in, say, Budapest or Bangkok, has nothing to do with the individual qualities of either, but everything to do with how well off all their customers and suppliers are.

Power and Mattering
Your power determines your welfare. To the degree that you do not have power, you are poor and frustrated. Maybe even homeless, hungry and ill-clothed. But such miseries are probably not the worst of the matter.

Being powerless means that you do not matter much; and that may be the worst feeling a human being can have. To matter to others is to have them think you are valuable, worthy of their respect and honour. When you matter to other people, they appreciate you and your services; they admire you; and when it is variously appropriate, they are grateful to you, sympathetic, empathic, caring, helpful, kind, loyal, faithful, loving. Even in routine interactions, people show that you matter to them (when you do), by being courteous, civil, cordial, gracious, tactful, considerate. (When they are the opposite of those ways, they are plainly showing that you do not matter to them, except perhaps negatively; and that is when they can make life hell.)

When other people treat you in those positive ways, your self-respect is reinforced, you know you matter; and there is probably no knowledge more gratifying to a human being than the knowledge of being valuable. You earn those treatments

Power, Behaviour, and Success

and messages by doing well things that other people consider important and that they know require skill, effort, self-discipline and similar qualities not always in great supply.

The rub, to repeat, is that the experiences which enable you to have the qualities necessary and sufficient to matter (to have power) are outside your control. And that is the fact of life to be emphasized when we think of the differences between people who objectively understand themselves and their world, and people who live under the illusion that their subjective experiences with power and mattering are enough for understanding.

Bargaining Power
Related to, but different from, power is bargaining power. Your power refers to your chances of getting what you want; your bargaining power refers to your chances of getting it on good terms, at little cost. In everyday speech, you get a good bargain when you get something at less cost than you might have expected.

Power and bargaining power are alike in that they are both great to the degree that other people are willing and able to do what you want, and there are many such other people and not many like you. But they are opposite to one another in two respects. If you want or need someone's compliance desperately, and if you are ready, willing, and able to do what he or she wants in return, you are likely to get what you want; but you are also likely to pay a big price for it. Your power is great, but your bargaining power is low.

And the other way around: if you really do not want the car or the employee very much and do not in fact have much money to spend on it or him or her, then you are not so likely to succeed; but *if* you do, it will be on very good terms for yourself.

You Are What Happened to You
The major point I have been emphasizing is that a major quality of people who are freed from the illusions that experience is enough for knowledge, is that they understand all

Experience versus Understanding

that. They understand that they are what happened to them. They understand that they have the determinants of their actions that they have, the determinants of their power that they have, and the determinants of their mattering that they have, because they had the experiences in various scripted games that they had.

And, of course, because other people in their environments had the experiences they had. People who do not know that, or deny it, or pretend it isn't true form one sort of dangerously mistaken person. For denial or ignorance entails the conception of oneself as divine: an uncaused god; self-made; owing nothing to anyone or anything. A miracle, no less.

Not many people articulate such a self-conception (the consequences would usually be unpleasant), but since denial of the facts leaves only that possibility, there are many tell-tale symptoms of any secret harbouring of the notion.

A central one is immodesty, or pride, in one of the old-fashioned senses in which pride was one of the seven deadly sins. That is the sense resulting in conceit, bragging, arrogance, pomposity, superciliousness. Other symptoms are touchiness, over-sensitivity, intolerance of criticism. ('Are they treating me as the sacred thing I am?') Those are repellent stances resulting from a combination of power and denial that the power is an outcome of historical happenstance. ('I owe my beauty to me.')

When the denial is combined with the opposite fate – with powerlessness – one possible unpleasant result is some form of self-abasement, self-hate, servility. One goes around apologizing for one's existence and cringing at one's looks, poverty, or lack of skill.

I have no suggestions about which is the more distasteful – the dumbness of arrogance or the stupidity of servility – although it is clear that the former is more dangerous. (It is coupled with power.)

Fully mature people – people with objective understanding – are neither arrogant nor servile, pompous nor self-abasing. They are simply realistic. They may feel lucky or unlucky, pleased or rueful about what they drew; maybe even thankful

Power, Behaviour, and Success

to or irritated with the people in their pasts who endowed them (saddled them) with the qualities they now have. But they do not brag and they do not whine.

It takes either ignorance or pretence to brag or whine about historical givens, which is why one of the bedrocks of maturity is understanding your present as your past.

Another bedrock is a sense of responsibility for your actions, even knowing that they are determined. That may sound oxymoronic, but it is not, as we will see below.

Your Behaviour and Power: Yours and Others
Mature people understand that people behave in accordance with the principle of the decision variables; and they succeed (or do not) in accordance with the principle of the power variables. There is one further understanding that people with objective understanding must have (because it is true and important); namely, an understanding of the relationship between the two sets of determinants: the determinants of power and the determinants of behaviour.

The relationship is not hard to understand. It can be put in two different ways. The first way is simply to notice again what your power is all about, and how it depends on other people's decisions. Your power refers to your ability to get other people to act as you want them to act. But their actions depend on the values of their decision variables. That is to say, then, that your power importantly depends on your willingness and ability to adapt yourself to their characters.

They are likely to act as you want them to act to the degree that you offer them things they value, and that they feel relatively deprived of. They are likely to act as you want them to act to the degree that they think doing so will get them the rewards you promise (or avoid the costs you threaten), as soon as they prefer, and at costs they think they can afford, compared to alternative ways in which they think they could get the same reward. They are likely to act as you want them to act to the degree that they think they have the abilities and resources to do so, and to the degree that they are willing.

Experience versus Understanding

The other people in your life are like any of your environments, in the sense that you must accommodate yourself to their nature. Your power depends importantly on the characters of the other people from whom you seek some compliance.

The other thing it depends on are the decision variables of all the other people who are also trying to elicit certain behaviour from those persons. It depends on your competitors, who are their alternative sources of reward; and it depends on the competitors of the people you are trying to influence, who are your alternative sources of compliance.

Your power, remember, is great to the degree that there are many other people who value your offerings; and to the degree that there are not many others making the same offering you are. The more competition you have, the less is your power; and the more competition they have, the more is your power.

Power, Competition, and Performance
We saw in Chapter 4 that the values of the decision variables (the elements of a person's characterological controls) are determined by cultural scripts and by the person's experiences in various culturally scripted games. We are now in a position to understand objectively how the nature of those experiences is affected by the power of the person and his or her environing others.

The reason a behavioural psychologist, or any animal trainer, can so readily shape the behaviour of pigeons or dogs is that he or she has so much power. The psychologist monopolizes the pigeon's supply of food and everything else the pigeon values. The psychologist has no competition, while the pigeon has no alternatives; and the psychologist doesn't need the pigeon's compliance nearly as badly as the pigeon needs the psychologist's. So it is hardly surprising that the pigeon ends up a dedicated circle pecker, or whatever the psychologist wants it to become.

So it is also between people. The reason it is relatively easy for adults to shape the behaviour and character of infants is that the power balance is so lopsided in favour of the adults.

Power, Behaviour, and Success

The reason it is so hard to reshape the character of an adult, or (God knows) a teenager, is that any would-be change agent has so much competition; and the adult in question so often can reward himself or herself internally. Imagine a psychologist whose pigeons have a dozen other sources of grain from competing psychologists (or fellow pigeon gang members), and really do not need the grain as much as they need the self-respect of Not Submitting to Authority Even If It Kills You.

We noted in Chapter 3 that some behaviour is immune to environmental influence simply because the environments are indifferent to *whatever* behaviour a person displays. Here we are adding that some environments are powerless to select certain behaviours over others, even if they care a lot.

The variable of competition points to another extremely important way of objectively comprehending the relationship between your (and other people's) power and your behaviour. Summarily, it is that your competitors significantly shape your behaviour.

Your cultural script tells you what, in your role, you are supposed to produce. (Automobiles? Home runs? Scientific knowledge? Plumbing repairs? Whatever.)

But how much? How well? How efficiently? At what cost?

Why, as well as possible, of course, if you are adequately to please the environing people whose compliance you seek. But what is 'adequately'? How well is 'as well as possible'?

You cannot know; and neither can the people to whom you are making your offers in return for their compliance, unless you and they have some comparative evidence of how well is possible.

That is the crucial point at which competition affects both your power and your behaviour. The more efficiently your competitors perform, the more efficiently you must perform.

The combination of the principle of behaviour and the principle of power yields a fundamental principle of human role performance: no one can perform as efficiently as possible in any role unless three conditions prevail. The first, of course,

Experience versus Understanding

is that the cultural script defining efficient performance be clear and the role player be up to date on its specifications. (Does 'efficiency' emphasize speed? Precision? Minimum costs? Reliability? Durability?)

The second condition is that the role player understand that efficient performance is necessary (even if it is not necessarily sufficient) for receiving the rewards hoped for. The third is that he or she understand that inefficient performance is sufficient for swift, certain, and high costs.

Those conditions entail, obviously, that the role player have competitors, so that the evaluators of his or her performance (customers, clients, employers, employees, patients, teachers, critics, audiences, voters, auditors) have some comparative evidence of what performance levels, at any given time, are possible. The competition, furthermore, must obviously be such that something significant is at stake for the competitors, something that can be lost if performance falls too low, and gained if it is high.

Those are the basic sociological reasons behind Lord Acton's famous aphorism that power corrupts, and absolute power corrupts absolutely. If you have something to offer that is highly valued by many other people, and they are willing and able to give you whatever you are demanding for it, and you have a monopoly of it, then you have a lot of power. Then, not only are you not likely ever to change your behaviour or your character, but no one – not even you – can ever know how much more efficiently you could perform, if pressed a little by a little competition (or pressed a lot by a lot of competition). Then there is nothing to prevent you from becoming ever more sloppy, negligent, lazy – inefficient. Corrupt.

We might as well say, as we will elaborate later, that security makes for complacency and non-change; and absolute security makes for insolence and smugness. In another context, it is what makes for spoiledness and arrogance.

That is why command economies and dictatorships are less efficient social institutions than market economies or democracies. But more on that later, including the conditions necessary to prevent markets and democracies from degenerating into monstrousness or idiocy (see Chapter 8).

The classical Greek injunction, 'Know thyself,' means above all, humanistically, to understand the general fact that your actions at any moment are determined by your character. That is the case for everyone, and in that sense to know thyself is to know something fundamental about everyone.

It is also to know about everyone (hence, about yourself) that her or his character is itself the product to date of his or her biography to date. One's character, or free will, is the outcome of all one's learning experiences in all the culturally scripted games one has been put through or allowed to wander through so far, as affected by the power of oneself and others – over which one has virtually no control. Those experiences determine the values of the variables which govern the probability that one will do anything at all, from the most wonderful through the most vile to the most ordinary.

Knowing those general facts obviously entails knowing also that everyone is as characterologically unique as everyone's fingerprints, because no one could possibly have had exactly the same experiences in exactly the same sequence as anyone else. (The absolutely limiting barrier to that is the fact that no one can know what it is like to have himself as an environing other.)

Knowing yourself and everyone else also means, humanistically, understanding the truth about your power and theirs. That truth is that your (and his and her) probability of faring well in life is determined by the interaction between the preferences and abilities you happened to get, and the preferences and abilities everyone else happened to get, including your competitors as well as your exchange partners.

Understanding and Choice
Understanding yourself and your fate in those ways does not dictate what you should declare life to be for; but it guarantees that whatever choice you make, you make with your eyes open

Experience versus Understanding

about why people act and fare the way they do. Your eyes should now be open to the following facts about yourself and everyone else:

1 You cannot know anything about anything except through the cultural definitions of it you have learned.
2 Your present notions of what is valuable, what you have to do to get it and keep it, what the odds are of succeeding, what other people are like, and what life is for, are what they are because you had the experiences you had with environing others whose power in relation to yours was what it was.
3 If those things had been otherwise, which they could have been, you would be otherwise.
4 The same is true about all those others out there.
5 Therefore, what you have up to the present thought about how society should be arranged – what the rules should be – has to be understood as not an inviolable criterion, but as a product either of someone's engineering in the past, or of accident.
6 You are now able to choose what sort of experiences you and other people, including all those still unborn, will have in the future, and therefore what their characters will be.
7 Since you can choose, you are responsible for the future of the species.

You also know fairly well, from all those experiences you have had, how your society is arranged now – what the rules are; and what the consequences of those rules are. In the next chapter I will sketch the nature of a society governed by humanistic rules. You have to choose.

Summary: The Theses of Chapter 5

The Nature of Power
Power is the probability of getting others to act as one wants them to act; and five variables determine how much one has.

Power, Behaviour, and Success

Game Scripts and Power
The values of those variables are also determined by the cultural scripts of the institutional games of life.

Power and Mattering
Mattering in human life, and power, come to the same thing.

Bargaining Power
An important difference between power and bargaining power is that the more you want something, the greater is your power, other things being equal, and the less your bargaining power.

You Are What Happened to You
A crucial understanding to bring to all experiences is that everyone *is* the result of his or her experiences in prior cultural games.

Your behaviour and Power: Yours and Others
The relation between your power and other people's is a major determinant of you and your actions.

Power, Competition and Performance
Your competitors are related shapers of you.

Understanding and Choice
The more you understand about power, the greater is your responsibility for the consequences of your choices.

Part 2

Humanism and Individualism: Similarities and Differences

6

Virtues and Justice

Moral Virtues and Amino Acids
Both individualistic and humanistic worldviews prize the same moral virtues and despise the same deadly sins. This is hardly surprising; all viable human societies do so, for the reasons we noted in Chapter 3.

In workable human societies, interdependencies are culturally scripted in roles: parent-child, doctor-patient, employer-employee, salesperson-customer, friend-friend, and millions of others. A simple but vivid way to remind yourself of the necessity of such role scripts is to imagine, or remember, occasions in which there weren't any. On such occasions, you literally do not know what to do, and must circle the other person with some wariness until you can discover, or invent, a role scenario into which you can fit the relationship. Crusoe's first encounter with Friday will do for an example; and the children in William Golding's *Lord of the Flies* will do to illustrate how easy it is for role scripts to be lost.

Role scripts specify how much of what each role player is supposed to try to get from and provide to the other; how much of what each is supposed not to try to get or give; and how those exchanges are supposed to be conducted. ('Capitalistically?' 'Communistically?' 'Altruistically?') It is the existence of such

Experience versus Understanding

scripts that generates the ever-present possibility of frustration. Hell is other people deviating from the scripts you think should apply. Or else it is other people insisting that you conform to scripts that hamper your egocentricity – as, of course, it is precisely the function of scripts to do.

Role scripts do for people what amino acids do for social insects. In the one case, the structure and operation of cultural shoulds and should nots define and regulate interdependencies; in the other case, genetic programmes do. The indispensability of the role scripts, combined with their fragility and tenuousness, as compared to the rigidity of genetic instructions, accounts for the development in all human societies of essentially the same conceptions of basic moral virtues and deadly sins.

The reason is that a necessary condition (not a sufficient one, as we will see, but definitely a necessary one) for minimizing frustrations and optimizing social integration is that people do what their roles say they should do. Otherwise, no one knows what to expect from anyone else; and no one can relax his wariness enough to get on with the job – the nature of which, in fact, no one can know for sure. If, to invent a random example, you think about entering my dental surgery with your toothache but cannot know whether I'll fix your tooth, rape you, sell you cocaine, cut your hair, trim your toenails, or a thousand other things, you can hardly get the day started.

To some minimum degree, it has to be the case that most people most of the time play by the rules of the game they announce themselves as playing: dentistry, baseball, lovemaking, parenting, or whatever. There are, however, always temptations and opportunities for role players not to do so. Playing by the rules is always incompatible with spontaneity and impulsiveness, by definition. It is often boring, fatiguing, and inhibiting; and playing any one role nearly always requires you to repress the worries or pleasures associated with others. (As my dentist, you are not supposed to be preoccupied with the sickness of your daughter or the sexiness of your lover, let alone the machinations of your broker.) Many roles involve

Virtues and Justice

risk, uncertainty, and danger, and entail temptations to panic and flee. All roles entail temptations to cheat; that is, not to conform to the rules; else there would be no need for the rules.

As we noted earlier, there is no rule in any society saying, 'Thou shalt eat what tasteth good to thee,' because there is no need for it. There are many rules saying not to do that, however, under various circumstances. If there is a rule, you may be sure there are motivations not to do what the rule commands. Cheating is always beneficial to the cheater in the short term, if he or she can get away with it.

Which is precisely why the same basic moral virtues are so highly prized in all societies, and the same things are regarded as deadly sins, no matter other dimensions of cultural relativity. Aristotle's famous eight moral virtues all say, in effect, 'Do not let down the people who rely on you to do what you promise to do by virtue of being in the role you are in:' be truthful in your implied promises; have courage to continue even in the face of danger; be just, gentle, temperate, and liberal in your demands and your offerings (do not unfairly deprive, strain, surfeit, or reject those who depend on you); be loyal in your friendships; and, withal, play your role 'high mindedly', not with selfish exploitation.

The classical seven deadly sins similarly highlight the temptations that seduce people into cheating in one way or another on their role duties – and hence become hell for other people. Lust, greed, anger, envy, sloth, pride, and gluttony represent (face it) very attractive activities; never mind those repulsive labels.

INTEGRITY. Put summarily, in every human society the moral virtue that is basic to all others and to the very operation of the society is integrity. Integrity amounts simply to playing by the rules of whatever game you announce yourself as playing. It is the quality of allowing others to count on your doing what the role you announce yourself as playing says you will do.

Integrity incorporates the virtues of honesty (you won't lie

Experience versus Understanding

just because it will give you an edge at the moment – which it always might), courage (you won't quit your role just because some danger threatens), gameness (you won't quit just because you're tired and aching), temperance (you won't get too high to do the job right), and most of the other qualities everyone always admires.

Integrity means not doing any of the many things it is always tempting for human beings to do. Temptations are the benefits of betraying integrity, and they are always present. (To repeat, if it weren't beneficial to be immoral, there would be no need for morals.)

This is a point at which the individualistic ethos, which prizes integrity as much as does a humanistic ethos, none the less generates a special difficulty. For the most general temptation to betray integrity is the temptation to give precedence to the welfare of your favourite subsystem, rather than the species as a whole, such as your tribe, nation, race, state, province, community – or self. We see instances of yieldings in the frequent wavings of banners of states' rights, national sovereignty, local home rule, ethnic purity, or individual or corporate 'privacy'.

Several specific manifestations of that general temptation should be especially noted.

One consists of a variety of enticements not to be as productive a contributor as you could be. Laziness, negligence, sloppiness, malingering, or disdaining work that is 'beneath you', comprise one common way of exploiting other people by reneging on your promise (as an interdependent member of a larger society) to do what you can as well as you can. Robbing, stealing, lying, and other varieties of blatant cheating are other familiar forms. Bullying, extorting, conning, or otherwise failing to respect other people are always tempting ways of furthering personal (or other subsystem) welfare at the sacrifice of integrity as a member of a larger system which includes the victims.

The Insufficiency of Virtues
Another important difference between the two major belief

Virtues and Justice

systems in this connection is that, for individualism, those individual virtues tend to be the end of the matter. Good people are people who are personally virtuous. While humanism agrees, that is far from the end of the matter.

Our capacity to admire virtuous behaviour – whether instrumentally or morally virtuous – is indispensable if people are to be virtuous. We want the people with whom we are interdependent to be intelligent and courageous, skilful and loyal, and so on; and they are the more likely to develop those qualities the more ready we are to admire and applaud them for doing so. But all the instrumental virtues and all the moral virtues may be seen equally (along with all the vices also) among Trojans, Greeks, Confederates, Unionists, Indians, Jews, Arabs, Protestants, Catholics, Muslims, Hindus, Blacks and Whites.

The bait of admirable individual qualities is extremely seductive to people with the admirable capacity to admire. Which is why that capacity is no good at all as the sole basis for evaluation. You need in addition some conception of a purpose and some conception of the rules you think will be effective means for achieving it. Courageous, loyal, gallant, skilful, clever, and similar behaviours need to be evaluated in terms of their significance for those rules and purposes before basing action on any admiration for them. Many Nazis were courageous, intelligent, loyal and so on; but that is not enough. Humanistically, we are led always to evaluate actions in terms of their long-range consequences for humanity.

Justice
The vital moral principle of justice also receives sharply different formulations under individualism and humanism, although it is necessarily prized in each. To understand its necessity and its differing definitions, we must, again, get some distance from our immediate experiences.

THE NEED FOR JUSTICE. Your power determines your welfare and sense of mattering; and the prevailing cultural scripts determine the distribution of the determinants of power. Are

Experience versus Understanding

there any principles for evaluating the desirability of the scripts?

'Desirability' in this case is translatable as 'justice'; and, as usual, evaluations depend on initial assumptions about purpose. I noted earlier that the basic moral virtue of integrity is the character trait of playing by the rules of whatever game you announce yourself as playing. Co-ordination of interdependent individuals requires as a minimum that they be controlled by that morality. But people are likely to play by the rules, in turn, only to the degree that they think the rules are fair, or just.

What does that mean? What are 'just' or 'fair' rules; and why is fairness so important?

One obvious meaning of fairness is that the rules of the game, whatever they are, be enforced impartially. The rules must be the same for everyone involved, the sanctions for violating them must be the same for everyone, and the probabilities of having to pay the sanctions must be the same for everyone. An ideal example, at least of the first two characteristics, as Thomas Schelling (1971) once pointed out, is the wholly impersonal and impartial traffic light. It is magnificently indifferent to any special pleading by any motorists, to any of their personal qualities or to anything about them. It is red for one direction and green for another for specified periods of time, and then reverses the opportunities; and does not even know the meaning of favouritism or discrimination.

It is not nearly enough, however, that the rules be enforced equally; it is also necessary that the rules themselves be considered fair.

What does it mean to speak of fair and unfair *rules*? What is the standard applied to rules to test their fairness? Let us approach the question in our customary way with an example.

You are considering whether to play a game in which you pay a dollar to choose one of ten boxes. One of the boxes contains a thousand dollars; the rest are empty. The probable benefit to you of playing the game is $.1 \times \$1{,}000 = \$100$; so you rationally decide to do that X of paying the dollar, and are just about to do so. At that moment, you learn that for the same cost,

Virtues and Justice

the game director is allowing me to choose one from ten boxes, *nine* of which contain $1,000, the tenth being empty.

An objective opportunity that was satisfactory to you a moment ago has suddenly become unsatisfactory; and the only difference is your knowledge that I have a better chance. Fairness has entered the picture, and you will demand to know why we are being treated unequally. And that question points to the standard of fairness. It is that either the rules must treat people equally, or there must be a morally satisfactory reason for treating them unequally.

Put another way, the basic principle of fairness is that the burden of proof is on the person who would defend a rule denying equal treatment.

What sort of reasons might be satisfactory? How might one sustain the burden of proof?

Consider the same example. Suppose that ten minutes earlier you and I had each paid a dollar to play a different game. The rules of that game were that five boxes contained the message, 'You have just won the right to play a game in which you have a ninety per cent chance of winning $1,000.' The other five boxes contained the message, 'You have just won the right to play a game in which you have a ten per cent chance of winning $1,000.' I had happened to choose one of the first five boxes; you had chosen one of the second.

What a moment before may have seemed unfair, now seems fair, because our unequal chances had resulted from equal chances.

WHY IS FAIRNESS SO IMPORTANT? Suppose they had not resulted from equal chances. Suppose the explanation of why you were given a ten per cent chance and I was given a ninety per cent chance was that the game director and I had the same religion, that's all; and if you don't like it, shut up and go back where you came from.

What is the cost to you of my having a better chance in that second case, which you do not pay in the first case? You cannot answer that the cost is that you are put at a disadvantage – are handicapped – in relation to me, because you are at exactly the

Experience versus Understanding

same disadvantage whether my better chance came from equal chances or from religious discrimination.

The extra cost is respect. Fair rules may well lead to unequal outcomes, or even unequal chances; but unfair rules lead to those results in a manner that is insulting. When you are treated unfairly, you are being told that you do not deserve an equal chance and that we who treat you unfairly are so contemptuous of you and your power that we do not even worry about your interest in punishing us. You do not matter to us.

To insult someone, the dictionary tells us, is to treat him or her 'insolently, or with contemptuous rudeness'. That is why fairness or justice is so vital an ingredient in co-ordinating interdependent persons. People can put up with inequalities, even inequalities of chances, so long as they believe they are receiving equal respect.

EQUALITY OF RESPECT AS KEY. The test of the fairness of a rule is whether it treats everyone as equally respectable, as mattering equally, or on the contrary, insults some persons. What sorts of inequalities of treatment, then, are likely to be considered fair? We briefly considered above one fair ground of unequal treatment; namely, the ground that unequal chances in one activity result from equal chances in another.

Other grounds are possible. The basic principle involved has sometimes been labelled 'the normative power of facticity'. (Hans Kelsen, 1945). The phrase refers to the tendency for people to consider aspects of life which seem factually inevitable as also moral, proper, just, fair.

In the context of fairness and justice, George C Homans (1974: pp 249–50) stated the principle nicely: 'The rule of distributive justice is a statement of what ought to be, and what people say ought to be is determined in the long run and with some lag by what they find in fact to be the case.'

Now, all the foregoing considerations apply equally to societies attempting to operate by individualistic scripts about purpose and to those attempting to operate by humanistic scripts. But the two different scripts impose on people very different kinds of specifications of the general principle.

Virtues and Justice

LIFE AS AN ECOLOGY OF GAMES. In the aggregate, according to the individualistic view, human life is simply an 'ecology of games', in Norton Long's famous phrase (1958). His analogy is to the fact that all the flora and fauna in a non-human ecosystem have their own genetically scripted games, but there is no super-game of the whole system. To be sure, out of all the interactions of special game players (rabbits, foxes, grasses) the over-all ecosystem takes on a certain shape and there is a certain distribution of everything anyone might be interested in. For example, there are a certain number of foxes and a certain number of rabbits and a certain amount of grass, all in a certain degree of health.

However, none of the players in all those genetically scripted games even knows about all that, let alone has any notion of how it all 'should' turn out. All that can be said is that the way things turn out is the way they should turn out because that is the way they did turn out.

THE INDIVIDUALISTIC VIEW OF HUMAN LIFE. On the individualistic cultural assumption, human life is like a natural ecosystem. People draw from the genetic roulette wheel what they draw, and from the experiential dice what the dice turn up, and that is that. And since it was all chance, it was all fair. Those chance events determine what specific games evolve (baseball? cricket? science? magic?), and what parts, if any, each person will play in any of them.

Those become the facts of your life, and it is up to you to make the best you can of them for yourself. True, you did not ask for any of it, but neither did any fox or rabbit. Out of your and my and everyone's strictly selfish strivings, there will emerge a certain shape of the social system, and a certain distribution of rewards; but it is morally wrong, pointless, and inefficient for anyone to try to guide the process towards any ideal end state. In its purest form, this could be the literal 'ecosystem' Hobbes and Locke called the 'State of Nature'. As Hobbes famously remarked, given the facts of interdependence, the raw form of the selfish premise could make individual lives nasty and short.

Experience versus Understanding

Many eighteenth-century philosophers imagined that rational self-interested human beings in such a state of nature would evolve a 'social contract' ameliorating the rawness. As a more recent philosopher, Robert Nozick (1974), argues the case, a 'minimal state' would evolve, or would be more or less consciously agreed to. It would be simply a 'night watchman' state, restricting itself to the prevention of force and fraud among its members.

JUSTICE UNDER SELFISHNESS. Nozick is probably the most distinguished contemporary exponent of this point of view, especially with respect to the special conception of justice it entails. As he says, in this view the very idea of worrying about the justice of any outcome of the ecological process is incomprehensible. 'Why,' he asks (1974: p 158), 'must differences be justified? Why think we must change, remedy, or compensate for any inequalities...?'

The only reasonable principle of justice derivable from individualism, says Nozick (p 158), is 'To each according to how much he benefits others who have the resources to benefit those who benefit them.' This is the same as saying that you are justly entitled to what your power gets you.

For example, with respect to any such idea as 'unfair discrimination' on the basis of race or sex or whatever, Nozick argues (correctly, of course, given the premise of individualism) that the issue is a non-problem. The only rights people have are the rights to do what they want with the resources their power has brought them. 'No one has a right to something,' he says (such as a job, or admission to a restaurant, or housing, or whatever), 'whose realization requires certain uses of things and activities that other people have rights and entitlements over' (p 23).

If I have acquired something without the use of force or fraud, I should have the right to let you have access to it, or sell it or rent it to you, as I please, according to this doctrine. If you do not please me for any reason, that is too bad for you, but morally proper for me. No one can have any general right to any special level of welfare, simply because 'people's particular

Virtues and Justice

rights over things fill the space of rights, leaving no room for general rights to be in a certain material condition.'

The Humanistic Conception of Justice
The humanistic specification of the general principles of justice is very different. To begin with, people who understand the facts of their lives independently of their immediate experiences know that there are two sets of things that people find in fact to be the case, which are crucial to sentiments of fairness. They are the facts of the determinants of actions and the facts of power.

FAIRNESS AND THE DECISION VARIABLES. Concerning the first set, the facts are these:

1 People do not willingly do things unless they think the rewards will outweigh the costs.
2 The greater the costs of doing something, the greater must be the rewards if people are to do it.
3 The riskier an undertaking, the greater must be the possible rewards if people are to undertake it.
4 The longer the time interval between doing something and getting rewarded for it, the greater must be the probability of getting the reward.
5 You can't get people to do things they don't have the resources for doing.

Since those are facts, most people in the long run come to recognize them as facts; and therefore, in the long run, come to perceive them as principles of justice. That is to say, they come to recognize it as a rule of fairness ('it's only fair') that people who pay similar costs, take similar risks, and make similar investments should receive similar rewards; and people who are dissimilar in those respects should receive dissimilar rewards.

Let us refer to all the costs, risks, and time and resources you and I invest in an action for the sake of some reward, as our 'inputs'. Then we can say, following George C Homans (1974:

Experience versus Understanding

p 249) and J Stacey Adams (1965), that fairness prevails between you and me to the degree that –

$$\frac{\text{Your Rewards}}{\text{Your Inputs}} = \frac{\text{My Rewards}}{\text{My Inputs}}$$

Fairness, in other words, does not require that you and I receive the same rewards, or take the same risks, or pay the same costs, and so on. It only requires that if you paid more costs or took greater risks than I did, then your rewards ought to be proportionately greater. Put very simply: if I want you to do something that is costly and risky, it's only fair that I reward you proportionately. And, very importantly, the other way around: if you refuse to pay any costs, take any risks, or make any investments, you have no claim on rewards from me.

When the ratio of rewards to inputs are not equal, one person is often said to be 'exploiting' the other; or at least to be benefiting from the exploitation of the other. Thus, I am being exploited and you are benefiting from it to the degree that your rewards divided by your inputs are greater than my rewards divided by my inputs. The injustice in your favour exists, whether this case came about because you and I got the same rewards even though your inputs were less, or because you got more rewards even though our inputs were the same.

FAIRNESS AND THE POWER VARIABLES. The basic fact about power, as we saw in Chapter 3, is that a person's power is a function of the match between the values of his or her decision variables, and those of other people. Thus, it is not just any old inputs you must make in order to elicit rewarding responses from other people. You must offer inputs that others value. Furthermore, those others must have decision variables that motivate and enable them to give you the rewards; and the rules of the game must be such that they cannot wilfully just get rid of you. They must deal with you.

At any given time, the nature of such matches is given. That

Virtues and Justice

is, everyone's offerings are what they are; everyone else's valuations of them are what they are; everyone's motives and empowerments are what they are. (There are a certain number of poor people and rich people, failures and successes, losers and winners, discontent and contentment.) And all those things are the way they are for certain reasons. The reasons, as we saw in Chapter 3, are partly the genetic structures of everyone, and partly the nature of the game experiences in which everyone had learned whatever he or she had learned up to that given time.

At any given time, things are the way they are because things were the way they were. Should anything be done about them; and if so, what? That depends on whether your fundamental world view is individualistic or humanistic. If it is individualistic, no, because however things are, that is the way individual self-seeking made them; and that is the way things should be. If your initial declaration is humanistic, it all depends on how fair it all is. If it isn't fair, indemnifications are in order; and social institutions which had resulted in the unfairness need to be improved.

Being Honest
At the very minimum, one might hope for at least an honest recognition of the consequences of alternative choices one can make, and an explicit acceptance of the costs of the choices. As I write, the Republican Party has taken control of Congress in the mid-term elections of 1994; and there is an increase in the talk that always goes on about taxes, welfare, budget balancing, and the like. Hardly any of it honestly states the fundamental issues. They can be stated quite simply as follows:

Call all the consumers goods and services that people actually buy in a given year, TTB (The Things Bought). Producing them requires certain resources – labour, equipment, land, capital funds. Call all the goods and services that could otherwise have been produced with those resources, TTF (The Things Forgone). Obviously, the real cost of TTB is TTF. (The real cost to you of the movie you paid to see is all the movies you are therefore not seeing at that time.)

Experience versus Understanding

Consider some of the things included in TTF. They are (among other things):

1 High enough ratios of teachers and related nurturers of children to give children presently under-nurtured the attention and supervision they need to develop productive understandings, skills and values.
2 Physical surroundings and related physical ingredients (nutrition, space, books, equipment, safety) necessary for such development.
3 Support and training for presently alienated unempowered, un-oriented adults.

There are certain observable consequences of forgoing TTF. They include the physical squalor of central cities and rural slums, and all the human casualties manifested in crime, addiction, despair, violence. Those pathologies are part of the costs of TTB.

Now, there is nothing necessarily 'wrong' with any of that. 'Wrongness' depends on the purposes you declare. Everything costs something; and if the things forgone were not forgone – if they became The Things Bought, instead – then, obviously, some of the things now bought would become things forgone. There is no escaping that everything costs something.

What there is that is terribly wrong with the present situation in the United States, by almost anyone's conception of purpose, is the seeming refusal to accept all that. What is wrong is the habit of choosing TTB and then complaining about the costs: about the consequences of TTF.

Often, indeed, there is more than complaining. There is rage that the refusal to do what is necessary to avoid certain consequences produces those consequences. Which is infantile, in the simplest technical sense.

What Americans need to do, if they do not want to change TTB (*and* if they do not want to be futilely infantile) is to learn to say: 'Yes, yes; we know there will be casualties of our individualistic, ecological decisions. Of course, there will be. Everything costs something – we know that. We accept the

Virtues and Justice

squalor, crime, despair, and all the rest of it as the cost of our lifestyles. If we put everyone in individualistic competition with everyone else for power, we will get Bach and Barnum, Einstein and Hitler, Mozart and rap, torture and Amnesty International, saints and sinners. We know it; we buy it; now let's just get on with it.'

BEING SURE. It is at least possible, however, that if certain other things about being human were understood better, Americans would choose not to say that. That is, they would choose to change. I now get on with the effort to get readers to understand those certain other things; so they can at least be sure about their choices.

Summary: The Theses of Chapter 6

Moral Virtues and Amino Acids
Human beings rely on morals to elicit the society-enhancing behaviours that are elicited in social insects by DNA.

The Insufficiency of Virtues
Individual virtues such as intelligence or courage are not sufficient to evaluate actions; they are common to saints and sinners.

Justice
The need for justice: justice is the major quality of rules that motivates people to obey them.

Why is fairness so important? People think that fairness requires equality of treatments, unless inequality can be justified in terms of equality of respect. Unequal treatments can be justified if they maintain equality of respect.

Life as an ecology of games: A possible justification of unequal treatments is that they result from the same operation of blind chance as prevails in a woodland.

The individualistic view of life: Pure individualism regards human social life as an instance of the ecological principles.

Justice under selfishness: Robert Nozick. 'To each according

Experience versus Understanding

to his ability to benefit those who have the resources to benefit those who benefit them.'

The Humanistic Conception of Justice
Justice requires equality of respect.

Fairness and the decision variables: fairness prevails when the ratios of people's rewards to their costs and risks are equal.

Fairness and the power variables: fairness requires that people be equally empowered, or compensated for unequal empowerments.

Being Honest
The great costs of the individualistic view do not compel humanism; but honesty at least requires their up-front acceptance. An acceptance speech is supplied.

7

The Problem of Losers

Under any definition of purpose, some individuals will be more successful, because more powerful, than others. The special thrust of the individualistic view, as we have seen, is to add that the less successful are 'losers,' and are solely responsible for their relative or absolute failures, and must make the best of it. It is their own fault, just as the success of the winners is a matter of their own virtues.

In one sense, of course, we must agree. In so far as the losers (and the winners) have subscribed to the individualistic rules of the game, they have agreed to abide by the consequences of those rules, which include the consequence that there will be winners and losers, whose success or failure will be culturally ruled as their own doing.

Keeping Losers in the Game
As Erving Goffman once pointed out, the situation has many of the features of a classical 'confidence game' ('On Cooling the Mark Out', 1962. See also the movie, *The Sting*.) In con games, a team of con artists gain the confidence of a victim, the 'mark', and generously permit him to join them in an undertaking that will make them all rich. The undertaking is usually an illegal or at least a shady one, but, they persuade the mark, a safe one. The mark's role is simply to supply the necessary capital, which

Experience versus Understanding

usually comes to as much money as the mark can beg, borrow, and steal. The mark turns over the money; the con artists apply the sting; and flee, leaving the mark holding the (empty) bag and, naturally, stunned by the enormity of what has happened to him.

There is no telling what damage marks so ruined might do in their emotional despair and rage: kill, commit suicide, stay drunk, become insane enough to go to the police, rampage – make some sort of scene that could upset the routine of the con artists. To guard against such unseemly reactions, one of the con artists not known by the mark to be a member of the gang, sometimes stays behind to sympathize, commiserate, support, and calm down the mark; help him adjust to his loss of power and self-respect. Cool him out.

The analogy is obvious enough. Under the individualistic script, millions of people invest a lot, thinking they will get rich in some fashion, but have some of the many things go wrong for them that can so easily go wrong for people, so they end up relatively powerless. Millions of people have practised early to bed and early to rise and all the other virtues, and wound up neither healthy nor wealthy nor wise, but rather poor, rejected, and bewildered. They are losers; and we do not need to postulate any evil con artists, whether gods or a ruling class, pulling the strings to recognize that those who benefit from the arrangements in which the losers lost, had better worry a little about how the latter might react. They may need those marks to be cooled out.

As in a literal con game, what is needed is for losers of all degrees to continue playing their roles anyway, at least enough, as we have noted, to keep the goods and services flowing. For that, viable societies have always had some forms of bread and circuses; both literal and figurative opiates of the masses; police forces; and sacred and secular psychotherapists. Many of the last-named in modern societies have often been accused by radical critics of being the winners' coolers, secular counterparts of priests who help many losers to accept their lot instead of smashing things by assuring them that their rewards will come by and by. 'Rage here in the office, but pull yourself together and cool it outside,' may, in fact, be the bottom line message of many therapists.

Such explicit messages are not, however, really needed. The numbing distractions of contemporary television, movies, radio, spectator sports, and newspaper entertainments seem to work, for the most part, to hold the critical games together well enough. It may be that the cooling effect of those endless outpourings, whose continued existence is otherwise puzzling, is adequate compensation for the pointlessness of the dominant culture.

Still, many of the losers refuse to be cooled out. They have internalized too strongly the cultural definitions that say 'Win!' and 'Use whatever means work.' Among the more familiar and unpleasant means that often seem promising to people who might otherwise be losers are crime, corruption, negligence, fraud, gambling, assault and similar stratagems. The sense in which those may be rational choices by some persons has been made clear by Thomas Schelling (1963):

> The ordinary healthy high school graduate of slightly below average intelligence, has to work fairly hard to produce more than $3,000 or $4,000 of value per year. [Schelling was writing in terms of 1963 prices.] But he could destroy a hundred times that much if he set his mind to it. Given an institutional arrangement in which he could generously abstain from destruction in return for a mere fraction of the value he might have destroyed, the boy clearly has a calling as an extortionist rather than as a mechanic or clerk.

Or a mugger, drug runner, embezzler, junk bond manipulator, pilferer from the company, tax cheat – and on through the endless examples in every daily paper.

The individualistic response to losers who become wrong-doers (or potential losers who become wrong-doers in an effort not to become losers) is to punish them. More police are hired, more prison sentences are made mandatory and more severe, more prisons are built, the death penalty is used more

Experience versus Understanding

frequently. Political campaigns are run on the issue of who is tougher on crime.

From a humanistic point of view, all that is exactly half right, at least in the sense that full understanding of the human condition includes the understanding that the costs of undesirable behaviour must be made greater and more certain than the benefits. But the full understanding also includes the understanding that the opportunities for desirable behaviour must be vividly present and their benefits must be greater and more certain than their costs. Not to include that latter understanding is one of the more pernicious results of failing to separate knowledge from immediate perceptions.

The Humanistic Interpretation: Assurance and Insurance
If the appropriate metaphor for individualism is an eco-system, an appropriate one for an important part of humanism might be an insurance pool. (An appropriate one for many collectivisms would be a concentration camp.)

Consider a simplified example of insurance principles.

The amount you have to pay into an automobile insurance pool every year, the 'premium,' depends mainly on two factors. One is the amount you insure for; that is, the amount you want to draw out of the pool if some lightning does strike you. The second is the number of people who get struck each year.

Suppose you and 999 other people join a pool to insure your cars. Suppose you all insure them for $10,000. Suppose the probability is that ten cars a year will be wrecked. Then 10 × $10,000 or $100,000 will be paid out each year; so you must each pay a hundred dollars a year in premiums (waiving, for the sake of the illustration, administrative costs). You pay and pay and pay, hoping you will never collect.

Suppose you want to reduce the cost of the insurance. There are two ways. One is to accept less indemnification for accidents; insure your car for only $5,000. The other is to reduce the probability of accidents. You might do this in many ways, such as having a rule of the game that no one may drive while drunk or drive over fifty-five miles an hour; that all drivers

The Problem of Losers

must pass various tests in order to be licensed; that all cars must have their brakes, tyres, etc inspected once a year; and so on.

You would be adopting rules requiring people to be prudent in various ways. All the rules would make automobile insurance less costly, and automobile ownership or use more costly, either financially or in terms of personal inconvenience. Both sets of costs are instances of the general category of maintenance costs: costs incurred in the present for the sake of avoiding larger costs in the future. One set consists of insurance maintenance costs (the premiums); the other, of risk-reducing maintenance costs (the prudence).

In a phrase, your choice is between the costs of assuring that accidents are unlikely, and the costs of insuring against the likelihood remaining. You cannot escape the costs; you can only choose between them.

Where should you stop in paying more and more risk-reducing maintenance costs (assurance costs) for the sake of paying lower insurance maintenance costs? Bear in mind that the more you fail to reduce the risks, the more you must pay to insure against them (unless you decide not to insure at all, a possible decision we will return to).

Why not stop at the point at which any further improvement in assurance (reduction in risk) would cost more than you would save in lower premiums for the amount of insurance you want to take out?

For example, suppose you could reduce the probability of cars being wrecked from ten to nine a year, by requiring all ears to have steel-belted radial tyres. Your insurance pool would then pay out only $9 \times \$10,000$ a year; and your premium would drop from a hundred to ninety dollars. Now suppose first that the extra cost of the radials per year is eight dollars. It makes sense to require the radials. Suppose, second, the extra cost of the radials is twelve dollars. It does not make sense.

The principle is that if your group decides it is uneconomical to assure everyone that accidents will not happen, then your group indemnifies the victims when accidents do happen. It is,

Experience versus Understanding

in an insurance pool, a matter of balancing the costs of assurance against the costs of insurance.

THE CHANCINESS OF POWER. Consider human life in general. You know that your power and everyone else's, and therefore that most priceless of goods, self-respect, can easily be reduced by chance events beyond your control. One kind of chance event is that you are struck by literal lightning, or such figurative lightnings as fire, a drunken driver, leukaemia, a heart attack, and so on. You know also that a second kind of chance event is to be struck by faulty or less-than-perfect genes, by the obsolescence of skills or equipment, by competitive overcrowding in your field, or by experiences in environments which do not equip you (or others on whom you are dependent) to make valued contributions. You know, in short, all the personally non-controllable elements of power we discussed earlier.

Humanism declares that it is as rational to pool the second kind of risks as it is the first.

Consider first the question of how much insurance it would be sensible for everyone to take out. I will not pretend to have any compelling answer, but you might consider at least five variables in making your decision. One is the cost to yourself and those you identify with and who are dependent on you of a power-lightning striking you. If you wind up unproductive for any of the many reasons that can make you unproductive, you have nothing and can do nothing for yourself or anyone; and you will have a bad time with your self-respect. A second is the cost to others of your being unproductive; you may be a drag on their charity. A third is the cost to yourself (and others you identify with) of others being unproductive. This could be a large cost because, remember, not only are you well off to the degree that you are powerful; you are well off to the degree that others are powerful. (This is a fact that people sometimes find hard to appreciate, so a reminder may be in order. The point is simply that your power is the probability that others will act as you want them to act. That, however, is partly determined by their willingness and ability to act that way, and by the intensity of their desires for what you offer in exchange – both of which variables help to determine their power. The more powerful others are in having the willingness and ability to act in ways you want, and the more they want what you offer, the more powerful they *and* you are.)

The fourth variable is the cost to you and everyone of people being unwilling to do their jobs wholeheartedly because they feel the rules of the game are unfair. 'Why should we work so hard for so little,' they might say, 'when we are not responsible for the lightnings that made our power so low?' Finally, fifth, even if implicit in the others, there is the fact that the higher you peg the indemnity to which people are entitled if they are victimized by power-lightnings, the more does it make sense to invest in assuring against power-lightnings. Put another way, it may be rational for you deliberately to set very high the penalty you must pay for not honouring people's rights to play productive roles. In doing so, you purposely construct for yourself and others an institutional environment which makes clear the rationality of providing experiences for people that will prevent them from adjusting to powerlessness and self-contempt in the anti-productive ways that make people unvaluable.

Suppose that, after considering those matters, you all decide to insure for a certain 'guaranteed annual income'. Every year, you all pay a certain amount in social insurance premiums, which now would probably be called taxes. In addition, you all pay a certain amount to provide for the members of your society the kinds of experiences that will make them powerful enough not to have to draw from the insurance pool. These would also be called taxes. You would always be choosing, through your political processes, how much tax to pay for assurance against power-lightnings, and how much to pay for insurance against the costs of your failure to provide the assurances.

How much to pay for each of those kinds of maintenance costs, insurance and assurance, will always have to be a matter of debate, and will depend importantly on the prevailing levels of scientific and technological know-how about enhancing people's power. It will also depend on the prevailing moral and aesthetic conceptions of what kinds of controls it is appropriate

Experience versus Understanding

to exercise over people's experiences, to assure their power. I return to some of those issues later.

At the moment, the point that cannot be over-emphasized is that, if you understand the facts about power, then you cannot fail to understand that when you observe someone who by the standards prevailing is less well off than he or she should be, you are observing the failure of existing social practices to have empowered that person adequately. Put another way, the amount of 'welfare' or 'charity' a person or group is thought to need, is a good measure of the inadequacy of the social practices which gave them that insufficient power. That is the case whatever declaration you make about human purpose; but what you do about it very much depends on whether you add to the facts a humanistic or an individualistic worldview.

Humanistically, you conclude that therefore everyone owes something to the persons deprived of adequate empowerment. Too poor people (which always means people with less power than is considered proper) are owed either (or both) power-enhancing treatments, or indemnities.

Then there arises the other question about such costs; namely, their allocation among individuals. Under individualistic rules, everyone is supposed to try to pay as small a share as his or her power permits. In the humanistic view, the facts of the determinants of power and of decisions (see Chapter 3) loom too loud and clear to permit that answer. They announce unmistakably that the powerful are the beneficiaries of the system's cultural scripts for regulating reproduction, education, training, competition, science, technology, art, and morality; and the most powerful are the ones who benefited most. Patently. So the humanistic answer, patently, is that people should pay whatever assurance and insurance costs are necessary, in proportion to the power with which the society endowed them.

A progressive income tax is simply a straightforward corollary of a humanistic worldview.[1]

---

[1] Or any other kind of tax: progressivity can be a feature of property taxes, sales taxes, or other kinds.

The Problem of Losers

The Two Traps
Behaving as humanistic environments to others always involves a never-easy steering between two traps. The traps are especially dangerous in the context of powerless people; that is, people who are losers in the distribution of empowerments; but it is well to understand the more general problem first.

On the one hand, at any given time there are all those billions of individuals with their unique, absolutely never-repeatable perceptions, imaginings, expectations, hopes, worries, fears, sufferings, pleasures, schemes, resentments, guilts, shames, prides, angers, envies, lusts, secrets. And none of those singular individual consciousnesses is ever fully or reliably accessible by any other of the billions. Novelists and dramatists try to give audiences some imaginative impression of what some of those inaccessible subjectivities might be like; and desirable people are always eager for the empathic experience. But it is always limited.

On the other hand are the millions of organizations and aggregations made up of culturally scripted roles. In any given period, each of the concrete individuals plays a specified role in at least several such organizations (a family – or two or more different families; a corporation; a church; a baseball team, a city; a nation; a club; and so on); and some people play roles in many. In his or her specialized role in any of those organizations, only a small fraction of the person's full self is relevant.

One trap is to forget the concreteness of the persons by becoming over-preoccupied with demanding excellent role-performances from them, without accepting the responsibility for providing the experiences necessary for them to perform excellently. The other is to become so involved in sympathy for their sorrows and emotions that we betray our responsibilities to the species by failing to hold them accountable for their role performances. The first is the trap of moral monstrousness; the second is the trap of moral idiocy.

Experience versus Understanding

THE TRAP OF MONSTROUSNESS. We are monsters, to begin with, to the degree that we encourage the production of people who are destined to be powerless.

Nearly everyone (except Nazis) recognized and recoiled from the monstrousness of the Nazi treatment of Jews and other people outside the Aryan collectivity. A particularly horrifying treatment was the deliberate 'medical' experimentation on minorities, to see how much pain and mutilation they could stand, and how they would react. The pain, misery, and humiliation of the victims was completely ignored in favour of the self-indulgence of the victimizers.

With that universally condemned case in mind, consider a set of cultural rules requiring the deliberate creation of infants with a certain probability that they will be genetically or congenitally handicapped, and with the certainty that they will be thrust into formative environments which will make them powerless and unwanted by their contemporaries.

The individualistic script which encourages people to do that (by insisting on everyone's right to do as he or she pleases and with an ecological conception of justice) is radically different from the collectivistic script of Nazism. It does not encourage people to revel in the miseries of the victims. The consequences, however, are none the less the production of people who were coerced into existence they would have begged not to have, had they been given a choice. Humanistically, that also is monstrous.

We are, further, monsters whenever we forget or ignore the concrete poignancies, heroisms, sufferings, and tragedies of individuals as they live out their short unasked-for lives, struggling for self-respect and power in the face of all the things that can – and sooner or later will – go wrong for them. Every person's story, as Herman Hesse (1965) said, is important, eternal, sacred because every person 'represents the unique, the very special and always significant point at which the world's phenomena intersect, only once in this way and never again.'

One thing all those unique intersections have in common is that each one acts out human needs to matter, and to feel, at

The Problem of Losers

least sometime, the epiphanies of loving and being loved, of admiring and being admired, of mattering and appreciating the mattering of others. And each one has felt failure and defeat and pain and anguish at some point in all those quests. Many respond with rage, despair, vengefulness, snobbery, whining, grovelling, alienation, anomie, depression, cruelty – the full range of pathos and of meanness that are also part of the human potential.

When we forget or ignore or fail to understand those hopes, struggles, pains, and reactions, we become monsters. When we look at other people, or read about them in history, and see only instruments or obstacles to our selves, or see only slobs who fall short of our standards, we skirt close to monsterness.

THE TRAP OF IDIOCY   On the other hand is the trap of moral idiocy.

While it is monstrous to give too short shrift to the unique preciousness of each person or to under-appreciate anyone's desirable behaviour, it is idiotic to give too short shrift to the standardized responsibility of each person or to condone anyone's undesirable behaviour.

It is possible (for many people, it is too tempting altogether) simply to wallow in the existential agonies of individual struggles for epiphanies and against frustrations – their own or others. Anti-monstrousness can too easily become self-pity and sentimentality, or the romantic self-expressiveness or anything-goes permissiveness that the 1960s excessed. It can also lead to an equally anti-humanistic cosseting of the victims of monstrousness. All such reactions are, just strictly speaking, idiotic.

They are idiotic because the very individual preciousness it is monstrous to ignore is a product of a culture-driven society that would be impossible to produce or maintain if individuals were not *also* made into responsible, accountable, answerable, evaluatable, instrumental units in a system of human beings much larger than any single person or any concrete set or list of persons.

Experience versus Understanding

That is why the temptation to accept disrespect from others or to yield to bullies (which may be safer than the alternative), or to wink at successful crooks (which may be more profitable) or cheer dashing desperadoes (which may be more fun) is wrong. It pollutes and weakens the moral universe. That is the same reason it is wrong to condone the malingering of charming good-for-nothings or adorable dependants or pitiable victims of injustice or bad luck: it infantilizes them and in so doing it deflates the moral universe. So does succumbing to the sad plight of people who insist on impoverishing themselves with the productive and reproductive scripts they insist it is their sovereign (or self-actualizing) right to follow.[2]

Pure altruism avoids monstrousness by making moral virtues only of pity, sympathy, kindness, mercy, forgiveness, self-sacrifice – which can be a kind of moral meltdown of standards in the name of Tender Loving Care. It leads (always to the horror of its wonderfully intentioned practitioners) to the idiocy of infantilization of everyone except, presumably, the hard-working core who do the infantilizing of the others. It sacrifices truth, efficiency, and beauty to what at the extreme is mawkishness.

What makes it idiotic is the reasonably clear fact that you cannot be long benefited by me if my heart bleeds too much – nor can the species get much understanding, power, justice, or art. Similarly, to indemnify the victims of injustice or bad luck is to restore a moral universe; but to confuse indemnifying with pampering is to re-destroy it.[3]

Somewhere along the line, a non sequitur became part of some versions of American liberalism. It is that, if people's bad behaviour is the result of their genes and their learning experiences, we must not make bad actors suffer for their

---

[2] Entirely apart from the economic dumbness, this is also why it is contemptible for bank and other leading agencies to lower critical standards of performance expectations for either venal or helpful motives, in lending money.

[3] The pathos of some of the potentially promising Liberation Movements of the 1960s is that the morally legitimate animus against certain parts of The Establishment devolved into a rejection of all objective standards of excellence in favour of celebrations of monstrous egocentricities and of idiotic bleeding-heartism.

bad behaviour. This has set back the cause of humanism considerably.

Determinism and Responsibility
The deep reason for the non sequitur probably lies in a widespread confusion about the relations among the concepts, determinism, free will, and responsibility – another instance of the mischief done by inadequate separation of thought from perception. We can clear a path through the thicket of confusion simply by emphasizing a few empirical and logical facts.

The most elemental fact of relevance is the one emphasized in Chapter 4. It is that people always act in the manner that seems to them at the time most likely to achieve what, in the circumstances as they see them, are the most important things to achieve. You cannot ask for more self-controlledness than that.

Actions are determined; and the determinants are such things as the persons' notions of importance, their interpretations of their circumstances, their conceptions of which actions will have what effects with what probabilities. Those mental states are that part of the self which gets expressed in the actions. Properly understood, then, to say that people's actions are determined in this manner is to say that people are always, necessarily, self-actualizing. What else could they actualize? The problem is, what is it *desirable* to actualize?

How did the mental states that actually determine actions come to be what they are? As we have seen, people learned them. They learned them by acting on the basis of previous mental states and having to adapt to the consequences of doing so. Sometimes the consequences were the ones the actors wanted, and then there was no reason for them to change. (The previous mental states were 're-inforced', as the psychologists say.) Sometimes they were not, and then something had to give – the preference, the expectation, or the strategy, for example.

Thus people learn to continue with old ambitions, preferences, expectations, assumptions, fears, misgivings, probability

Experience versus Understanding

estimates, tactics – or give them up and acquire new ones. Thus people change and become different persons, sometimes remarkably different.[4] Equally thus, people often do not change; they remain the same persons, no matter how bizarre or inefficient their behaviour may seem to outsiders. Everything depends on the feedback they get from their environments, and on their receptiveness to it.

Once these matters are understood, the seeming conflict between holding people responsible, on the one hand, and comprehending the ways in which they are determined, on the other, should disappear. The widespread notion that if people's actions are determined, they cannot be held responsible for them involves a simple, but enormously significant, error of reasoning.

The idea of holding you responsible refers to the question of how we should treat you after you have done something. Let you suffer the consequences of your action? Enjoy the consequences? Impose costs on you? Reward you? Shoot you?

The idea of the action's being determined refers to something utterly different; namely, the antecedent causes of your action.

Nothing we decide about how to treat you after you act can affect those antecedent causes that led you to act that way; and nothing about them can determine our selection of responses. Whatever the causes were, that is what they were, no matter what we do in response. The causes, that is to say, are constant over all the possible variety of our responses, and therefore cannot determine our choices about how to treat you. (If all the shirts I might wear today are white, then colour is constant over

---

[4] The pain of deep characterological change, and hence people's resistance to it even in the face of sharp frustrations, is suggested in one of Tony Kushner's powerful metaphors in *Perestroika*; Act III, scene v.

> God splits the skin with a jagged thumbnail from throat to belly and then plunges a huge filthy hand in; he grabs hold of your bloody tubes and they slip to evade his grasp, but he squeezes hard, he insists, he pulls and pulls till all your innards are ripped out and the pain! We can't even talk about that. And then he stuffs them back, dirty, tangled and torn. It's up to you to do the stitching.

The Problem of Losers

all my possible selections and cannot determine my choice of which one to wear.)

The only things that can determine our response to you are the values of *our* decision variables. (They, of course, were determined by past events in our lives; but that is very different from the past events in your life which caused you to act as you did.) We will respond to you on the basis of what we want you to learn, and on our notions of what is most likely to get you to learn that (including how much we hate you and want you to suffer, or how much we love you and want you to prosper). Those notions may be affected by our ideas about why you acted as you did, which may include our ideas about the biographical determinants of your decisions; but those matters still concern *our* decision, not yours.

Suppose you say to us something along the lines of what the young delinquents sing to Officer Krupke in *West Side Story*; namely, that they should be forgiven because it is only their 'bringin'-upke' that 'gets us outa hand.'

The response which logically, if not quite so tunefully, follows is, in effect, 'Yes, yes; we know the story. In fact, that is precisely the story we are going to use in our response. Since you had to do what you did because of certain variables, we are going to operate on those variables, by changing your mind about how the world works.'

The point here is such an important one, both for humanistic social policy and for the concept of desirable people, that it deserves to be put in still another way, for emphasis.

The fact that people are products of their pasts cannot mean that they are not responsible for their actions. In the first place, to be responsible means to be answerable, accountable. It means that you must give a good reason for your action; not merely an explanation of it. You must justify it; not recite what produced it.

Justification, however, is a moral term; not a scientific or technological one. Whether or not to hold you responsible for your action is a moral decision; and it has nothing to do with the purely intellectual or technological question of what caused you to engage in the action or what we

Experience versus Understanding

can do to affect your future behaviour.

The intellectual/technological issues of human behaviour do, on the other hand, have everything to do with the question of how we get you to stop doing some X and start doing some Y. We do it by using the same understanding and techniques we know led you to do the X and not do the Y.

What follows from the fact that you couldn't help X is (if we want you to do Y) that we must teach you that the world is different than you had thought: X entails costs you don't want to pay; Y entails benefits you would like to have; and you can do Y. And one of the ways to convince you that X entails costs is to impose the costs on you. A fairly sure way not to teach you that X entails costs is not to impose them on you.

Equally, one of the ways to convince you that Y brings benefits is to give you the benefits for Y. A very sure way to teach you that Y does not bring rewards is not to reward you for Y. And a really excellent way to teach you that Y is not necessary for the rewards is to let you have the rewards without Y. (We teach people effectively that productive work is not necessary for wealth or the high life by making wealth and the high life available to people who do not do productive work.)

Determinism and the Self

The fact that your actions are determined does not absolve you of responsibility for your behaviour. It absolves you of responsibility for many of your features (your height or susceptibility to cavities, for example), but not your behaviour.

Quite the contrary. The behavioural part of your formative history consisted precisely of the fact that everyone and everything in your many environments always and unavoidably held you responsible for your behaviour.

When you did not balance properly on your bicycle, the ground, in effect, held you personally responsible. That is how you learned to balance.

That is what learning means. It means acting in a certain way (because of your history up to that point), getting some response from others (or the ground), and recognizing that that

The Problem of Losers

act you did (*you* did) elicited that response from that environment.

That is what learning means whether you understand it or not. That is to say, *you* did all the acts you did, and *you* enjoyed or suffered the consequences. If you liked the consequences, you could do the act again; if you didn't, you could choose not to do it again. That is the case whether you realize it or not, deny it or not, complain about it or not, or whatever.

Many people seem to feel a contradiction between the realization, on the one hand, that a person's act at a given moment is determined by all that has gone before; and, on the other hand, that he or she must be held responsible for it. When a person who has done something wrong says, 'But I couldn't help it,' he or she is always telling the truth; and then, at first glance (which for too many people is also the last glance), it may seem somehow wrong to punish her or him.

The error of the first glance is a confusion between two very different questions: 'Why did she do that?' and 'What do we want to happen next and how do we cause it to happen?' The answer to the first question always is, 'She did it because her experiences taught her that that was probably the best thing to do in the circumstances as she understood them.'

The answer to the second question has nothing at all to do with that. It has to do with the future. First, we decide what we want from the person in the future; and then we say, in effect, 'If we want this person to go on doing what she just did, we reinforce her notion that that is the best action. If we don't, then we impose costs of some sort; and we make more desirable actions more available and more beneficial. We make the present *different* from the past *so as* to alter the future.'[5]

The point I am emphasizing is that a bed-rock of desirability, humanistically understood, is the *understanding* that that is the case. The recognition, acceptance, realization that it is.

---

[5] But bear always in mind the caveats mentioned in note 8 of Chapter 3 and note 4 of Chapter 4: people's characters can be formed to have internal rewarding mechanisms that make them virtually immune to further external changes (See also Chapter 8).

Experience versus Understanding

Summary: The Theses of Chapter 7

Keeping Losers in the Game
Under rules of individualism, losers pose problems like those of marks in confidence games: how do you keep them from spoiling the game?

The Humanistic Interpretation: Assurance and Insurance
Under humanistic rules, if you cannot assure people of adequate power, your duty is to insure them against the failure.

The chanciness of power: power is like health: since you might lose it accidentally, insurance makes good sense.)

The Two Traps
The trap of moral monstrousness: it is morally monstrous to encourage powerlessness or to exploit the powerless.

The trap of moral idiocy: it is morally idiotic not to demand of the less powerful what they can contribute.

Determinism and Responsibility
The fact that your behaviour is determined does not mean that you are not responsible for it. Quite the contrary.

Determinism and the Self
Your self, in fact, was *determined by* the degree to which you were held responsible for your actions.

8

Culture and Freedom

An American Army lieutenant who served in Vietnam during 1966 and 1967 wrote afterwards about the incidents of brutality and betrayal he had witnessed. Looking back on them, he said:

> You can't know it without being in it and once you're in it you can't get out of it. Nothing that anyone did made any sense, unless you were there, and then it was the only thing there was to do. It was hard to know who to blame. It was even harder to accept finally ... the fact that there was no one to blame, no adequate or effective scapegoat to take away the sins of the world ...[1]

One of the major theses of this book so far has been that *nothing* in human life makes any sense unless you are there in the culturally scripted games comprising your environment; and once you are in them, the only thing imaginable to do is to follow the programmes they prescribe for understanding and for mattering, in whatever ways they define understanding and mattering.

---

[1] Quoted by Jonathan Mirsky, 'Reconsidering Vietnam', *The New York Review*, 10 October 1991, p 46.

Experience versus Understanding

Intellectual understanding of that fact adds a further dimension to the issue of responsibility discussed earlier. It is that we are responsible not only for our own actions, but for a certain class of other people's actions also.

We are responsible for doing what our power permits to construct the societal environment which elicits the behaviour we consider desirable. And the obverse: if we get behaviour which we consider undesirable, we are responsible for it, to the degree that it has been elicited by any environment we condone.

At least, once you understand the argument so far, it becomes untenable to complain about behaviour which flows from cultural scripts you are unwilling to change. To summarize that argument briefly, there is no mystery in general about why people act in the ways they act. Those are the ways their experiences have taught them are most likely, given their power resources, to produce the results they have been taught to want.

The ways that are most likely are sometimes ways sharply constrained by bio-physical laws, as in such cases as handling sails on a sail boat, cooking a turkey, or performing gymnastics. Other ways are dictated by cultural laws, as in such cases as handling juries in a court room, purchasing a turkey in a market, or performing a play.

The second set of ways of acting is of most concern to us at the moment; and the point to be emphasized in that context is this: it is idle to think there is a choice between societies in which people's actions are controlled and societies in which they are not. People's actions are always controlled by the principles governing the responses of their environments.[2] The only choice – and it is a real and vital one – is *which* governing principles?

Freedom and Privilege
This point is so fundamental that it deserves to be elaborated in

---

[2] More strictly, at a given moment actions are determined by the *interaction* between internal purposes and perceptions on the one hand, and environmental responses on the other; but the internal elements are what they are because of previous interactions; and so on.

Culture and Freedom

another way. Consider the vastly important concept of freedom. Basic to all rational thinking about social affairs is the realization that freedom is not an end it is realistically possible to pursue. People cannot be free. As Alexander Herzen once put it, the Rousseauian notion that man is born to be free but is everywhere in chains, 'is as mad as to remark that "fish are born to fly, but everywhere they swim."'[3]

That is a fact which seems hard for many people fully to appreciate; but appreciation of it is indispensable.

Looking first at the single individual, once thoughts are adequately decentred from perceptions it is clear that he or she is not free to do anything not dictated by the inner controls comprising his or her character, which resulted from the evolutionary processes we reviewed in Chapter 1. You are not free to see the marks on this paper as anything but the English words you have been taught to define them as. Characters control.

Looking next at individuals in relation to one another, it is clear that people cannot be free for the simple reason that freedoms conflict with one another. Freedom is 'zero-sum', in the sense that the free-er you are to do certain things, the less free I am to do other things. If you are free to do X, I am not free from your doing it, or its consequences. If we add up all your positive freedoms, and subtract from them all the restrictions on my freedom that they imply, the sum is zero.

If you are free to behave in all the undesirable ways we have considered, the rest of us are not free from your effects; and vice versa. If you are free to buy certain goods at certain prices, we are not free to charge market prices. If you are to get free medical care or housing, many of us are obliged to pay for it. If you are entitled to know our secrets, we are not entitled to keep them. If they are free to have all those babies, no one is free from overpopulation. If you are free from searches as you board the plane, we are at risk from your guns or knives.

---

[3] Quoted by Ailen Kelly, 'Revealing Bakhtin', *The New York Review*, 24 September 1992, p 48.

Experience versus Understanding

What are usually called freedoms are in fact certain privileges of citizenship which are always contingent and always liable to withdrawal.

It is strictly inconceivable that even the precious privilege of individual bodily freedom to move about at will should not be wholly contingent on obeying a wide variety of rules; and it is strictly inconceivable that all the more particular privileges that make human life pleasant and worth living should not be contingent on obedience to certain particular rules.

At present in the United States, for example, we make the privilege of individual bodily freedom contingent on obeying many rules. It is instructive to review some of the more obvious and central ones.

You are free in the simple sense of not being in prison only if you have adequately met all of the following obligations of a citizen – with 'adequately' being defined by persons other than yourself:

1 You have been careful (so far as authorities know, at least) not to contribute to the death or injury of another person, or even to endanger anyone recklessly.

2 You have respected everyone else's property rights.

3 You have conscientiously refused to benefit yourself by taking advantage of a position of trust. (For example, you have not engaged in insider trading on the stock market, or unfairly co-operated with anyone to affect prices of anything in your favour.)

4 You have denied yourself certain pleasures that your society taboos, rather than purchase them. (Narcotics; the services of a prostitute.)

5 You have paid your fair share of collective social expenses in the form of various taxes.

6 You have not cheated on any of the many (*many*) rules about eligibility for playing various desirable roles, such as automobile driver or owner, doctor, teacher, pharmacist, barber...

7 You have honoured your society's standards of dress (you have not indecently exposed yourself, and you have

Culture and Freedom

worn a shirt and shoes in restaurants requiring them), and of deportment (you have not been drunk and disorderly, or defecated on the pavement, or emptied your rubbish in public parks, etc).

8 You have faithfully acted in the ways you either implicitly or explicitly signalled to other people that they could count on you to act. (You haven't conned people, or falsely or misleadingly advertised to them; or if you are a physician or lawyer or teacher, you haven't violated patients' or clients' or students' trust; or you haven't cheated on any of the rules of any games you agreed to play.)

In short, your sheer bodily freedom and the freedom to enjoy many of the general privileges of citizenship such as travelling from one place to another, are not really free at all. You can enjoy them only *if* you obey a very large number of quite specific rules. You do not, most of the time, feel most of the rules as onerous, unfair, or repressive; but that is only testimony to how efficiently the elders of your society have habituated you to them. It does not reduce the degree to which your freedom is sharply constrained by rules, or the degree to which your citizenship privileges are strictly contingent on your obedience. (And the other way around, of course: any feeling you have that various rules are onerous, unfair, or repressive is not testimony to the fact that they are rules; it is testimony to the failure of your elders to habituate you to them.)

Beyond sheer bodily freedom and general citizenship privileges, other more specific privileges that make life pleasant or even worth living are also contingent on performance of certain duties.

Call to mind what those specific privileges are. They include the food you eat, the beverages you drink, the clothes you wear, the electricity you use to see by or warm yourself by, music, movies, reading matter, beds to sleep on, trains or cars or buses to ride in ... and hundreds more. Think of how you get them. You get them only by making it worth someone's while to give them to you.

Experience versus Understanding

There are always several different ways of making it worth someone's while. The basic point I want to emphasize here, though, is that they are all different ways of making it worth while to someone else (not just to you) to act as you want him or her to act.

If you want any of the particular privileges I have just reminded you of, you must obey particular rules. Nothing is free. Whether you make it worth my while to give you food (for example), by paying me money for it (the capitalistic way, let us conventionally call it); or by showing me your requisition slip (the legal-bureaucratic or Communistic way); or by calling on my loyalty to you (the altruistic or familial way); or by persuading me that the food will make you a more productive worker (a co-operative way), there is always something you must give me in exchange. (Unless you take it by force, which exposes you to the loss of bodily freedom discussed above.)

The question can never be, how can people be made free? It can only be, what should the rules be, conformity to which is necessary for *which* privileges? It cannot be, 'Should there be rules?' It can only be, 'What should the rules be, eliminating *which* freedoms?'

It is the same with the cherished concept of free speech'.[4] Speech is always restricted by the rules of whatever institutional game is being played. A student in a college physics class who claims the right to express her political views in verse as an answer to the physics problem will be ejected and maybe jailed if she persists; and even in the much-celebrated marketplace of ideas, there are rules of libel, inciting to riot, and the like.

The absolutist First Amendment position that the value of unregulated speech outranks all other values makes sense only under one of two assumptions: that the speech has no consequences (it is babble, and the noise cannot even be heard by anyone); or that none of the consequences cost people with power anything they value very much. The matter is another

---

[4] Stanley Fish is the master analyst of this phenomenon. See *There's No Such Thing as Free Speech ... and It's a Good Thing Too* (1994).

Culture and Freedom

instance of the general principle that you cannot evaluate anything without some conception of its (desired) purpose. You cannot evaluate the proposition that 'This speech should be permitted (or not),' without some conception of the consequences either version would have, and some preference among those consequences.

And, of course, you cannot enforce your preference to permit it or not unless you have the necessary power.

In the rest of this chapter, I consider some basic aspects of the kinds of rules that are necessary to elicit desirable behaviour, including speech, humanistically defined.

Markets and Democracies
Lord Acton's famous aphorism, that power corrupts and absolute power corrupts absolutely, summarizes another of the bed-rock facts that successful human cultures must cope with. The potential danger of power to everyone, including the power holder, is that it can blind the power holder to the real nature of his or her environment. If you have absolute power over me, you are shielded from concern about the effects of your behaviour on me, and you are more likely than not, in the long run, to act in ways that destroy my willingness and/or ability to do what you want me to do.

Economic markets and political democracies are cultural developments providing the feedback that blocks the operation of Lord Acton's dictum.

MARKETS. For much of this century, a major argument was about the comparative merits of two sets of rules for pursuing the ideal of economic plenty. On the one hand, are the rules of the market; on the other hand, the rules of Socialism or Communism. I will focus on the market, which has clearly proved to be the most productive set of rules, and is the set now governing nearly all societies with any hope of approaching material plenty. Communism has proved the cogency of Lord Acton's formulation.

The first point to emphasize is that the market *is* a particular set of rules, enforced by the coercive power of a government,

Experience versus Understanding

granting certain privileges, rights, and freedoms, and emphatically curtailing others. A market system is not a place, and it is not freedom; it is a set of rules specifying who has *which* freedoms. The rules are these:

1 You own your own body and your skills, looks, energy, and knowledge; and you can do virtually anything you want with them, including renting them out and taking them to any place in the society you choose. To most western readers, it probably seems absurdly pedantic to say this; but it is a spectacularly significant rule, when contrasted with other possible, and often prevailing, rules such as those of slavery, serfdom, traditional caste and gender barriers (some of which still prevail in the west), and the rigid bureaucratic commands of Communism.

2 You may own any other useful resource, and rent, sell, or move it about as you choose, from personal belongings to tools, buildings, machinery, land, money, credit, patents, copyrights, or good names.

3 You may (indeed, you *should*, by the rules of the market game, just as you should make runs by the rules of baseball) rent or sell what you own to the persons or groups who will pay you most for them; that is, to the highest bidder.

4 In seeking to acquire any of those resources (from skills or knowledge to land or capital), you should buy or rent them from people who will charge you least: from the lowest bidder.

Those rules constitute an institutional maze or Skinner Box that causes people to be as inventive and energetic as they can be in using all their resources to please the consumers of their goods and services (which obviously includes efforts to shape their notions of what is pleasing, but these efforts, as with any would-be shapers, require acceptance of what they find pleasing to begin with). For the welfare of producers depends on such efforts; and the consumers' welfare depends on finding the most inventive, energetic, and efficiently pleasing producers possible. Moreover, as we emphasized earlier, competition among producers forces them to be as efficient as possible; and competition among consumers forces them to pay producers as much as necessary to keep them producing. (But, ideally, no more.)

Little wonder the market system triumphs, in the long run, over all *its* competitors, all of which substitute, in one way or another, mazes which reinforce complacency, rigidity, and submissiveness over drive and competition.[5]

DEMOCRACIES. Democracies are to polities as markets are to economies.

The central political question of societies is, Who should have what authority to decide what governments should do? (Just as the central question of economies is, Who should decide who should produce how much of what, and who should get it?)

The twentieth century debate over this question was between the rules of democracy and the rules of authoritarianism or totalitarianism. I will focus on the democratic answer, for the same reason I focused on the market in the economy case: dictatorships have failed, for Lord Acton's reason.

Before considering the democratic answer to the question, Who should decide what the government should do, we must get clear about the things a government *might* do. The insufficiently appreciated answer is that governments might do anything *any* organization might do. They can manufacture goods, do scientific research, tend the sick, educate the young, entertain the masses, bury the dead. Indeed, some government in some place at some time has done each of those things.

A government is the formal organization of the whole society.[6] It *can* do any of the sort of things just mentioned, if its

---

[5] Obviously, markets can be deformed towards bureaucracies when size or coercion or special political pleadings reduce competition; and then they lose their edge. Obviously also they may entail great humanistic costs. More on that later.

[6] The most lucid development of this understanding is by Alfred Kuhn, *The Logic of Social Systems*, Jossey-Bass, 1974, and *Unified Social Science*, Dorsey Press, 1975.

Experience versus Understanding

managers and directors choose; but there is one thing it must do, and only it can do it. That is to issue and enforce, coercively if necessary, the basic rules of the society. Governments, by definition, decide whether the rules of the economy will be market rules of a private economy, or bureaucratic rules of a Communist economy. They decide what people will be free to do and what they will not; and they decide whether to manufacture goods, carry out research, tend the sick, entertain the masses, bury the dead – or not. And they use force to carry out their decisions.

So it is rather important what the rules are that say who should decide what those rules should be. The basic rules of a democracy are these[7]:

1 At regular, fairly short, intervals, all adult citizens who care to do so decide in an election to which legislators and executives they will delegate the authority to make and enforce the rules until the next election.

2 Anyone who wishes (and can afford the cost) may try to persuade the voters to choose him or her.

3 The kind of rules the elected officials may make and enforce are specified in a constitution, which can itself be changed by special majorities of the adult citizens.

4 A vital part of the constitution are the guarantees of free speech, and freedom of assembly. These are vital, in order to assure that candidates and others can say what they want audiences and voters to know, and so that citizens can hear all the views and news they want to hear in order to understand their world.[8]

---

[7] All major democracies in the contemporary world are 'representative' democracies, rather than 'direct' democracies; so I will focus only on them. For an (unconvincing) argument as to why they will soon become direct democracies, see Brian Beedham, 'What Next for Democracy?', *The Economist*, 11 September 1993. Even more restrictively, I will focus on the particular form of democracy in the United States.

[8] In fact, it is the right to hear competing views and ideas that is the crucial right, and many debates about free speech could be clarified if this were widely appreciated.

Culture and Freedom

The parallels to a market are obvious: competing candidates offer to make rules they think will please most voters in their districts (or states or the nation), and customer-citizens choose the ones they prefer. The great and common principle of both markets and democracies is that the people who will be most affected by the power of producers (of goods or of rules) have the power to sanction the producers.

Other political systems consist of rules which give the authority to make and enforce rules to persons *other* than their consumers: to a hereditary elite, or to a self-perpetuating set of bureaucrats or priests, or to the toughest colonels.[9]

People's Wants and Human Needs

The built-in advantage that markets and democracies have over alternative systems is the advantage always given by competition. As I emphasized earlier, no producer of anything, from running a mile through automobile manufacturing to legislating can know whether he or she is performing as well as possible without comparison with someone else trying to do it better. And no fan or judge of running, consumer of automobiles, or citizen affected by laws can know whether he or she is being served as well as possible without the opportunity to shop around. The absence of competition in any area means the probable presence of complacency and arrogance – Lord Acton's corruption.

But it by no means follows that markets and democracies mean desirable societies, much as politicians and pundits in the later twentieth century like to pretend so, after the exposure of Communism's and totalitarianism's fatal flaws. Markets mean that consumers with money are likely to get what they want and consumers without are not; and democracies mean that citizens in majorities (or maybe even just pluralities, or maybe even just those who make large campaign contributions) are likely to get the rights and freedoms they want, and impose on others the duties and restrictions they want.

---

[9] Alfred Kuhn suggests that democracies should be understood as consumers' co-operatives, and various dictatorships, as producers' co-operatives.

Experience versus Understanding

Whether those outcomes are desirable or not depends on two other matters entirely: one's criteria of desirability, and the particular wants of the victors in the market competition for money, and the winners in the political competition for pluralities. If consumers want junk, the market guarantees that producers will happily provide it. If majorities or well-organized special interests want various repressions on others or various special privileges for themselves, democracies assure that legislators and executives will happily provide them.

To be sure, competitive producers of goods or laws try to persuade consumers and voters of what they should want (they should want the products the vendors are purveying); but it is not likely that they, with wise leadership, can, through market or democratic mechanisms, lead societies far from where they are at any given time. The reason should now be familiar. In markets and democracies, producers are rather in the position of psychologists trying to get pigeons to peck in certain ways, *when no psychologist has control over the pigeon's rewards and costs.*

It is not only, as reviewed above, that any psychologist must accept the pigeon's existing character as given (its wants, abilities, perceptions, past experiences, and so on), and can, at most, make only minor changes in its tactics. Worse than that, imagine a psychologist trying to influence a pigeon in a certain way when the pigeon has a dozen other psychologists offering better deals. The pigeon is not likely to change much.

(The *psychologists* are likely to change, at least in the sense of performing as excellently as they possibly can because of the competitive pressures they feel; but 'excellently' means, in such a case, reinforcing their clients' existing natures.)

Producers of goods and candidates for political office (and psychologists) can significantly change their recipients' behaviours just to the degree that the recipients' present behaviours are costing them more than they are benefiting them – as the recipients see the matter. Thus, political leaders such as Franklin D Roosevelt can effect large changes in society when large numbers of people perceive starkly that present rules are not overcoming a deep depression and are not avoiding a

Culture and Freedom

dreaded totalitarian enemy. Political leaders like Bill Clinton have a much harder time of it, not because *they* are so different but because their publics are in such different circumstances.

The psychoanalyst and social scientist, Erich Fromm, made the point nicely in his evocatively titled book, *Escape from Freedom*. Fromm was trying to understand the successful social transformations led by Martin Luther and Adolf Hitler; and concluded that such people could make great changes only when three conditions prevailed. First, people had to feel deeply frustrated and outraged by their circumstances under the existing rules; second, they had to feel bewildered and at a loss for what to do about it; and third, a leader had to appear who would say with great confidence, in effect, 'You are right to feel outraged. Here is the reason you are in trouble (it is someone else's fault). And here is how you must change in order to return to your rightful state.'

Then people will be happy to escape from the burden of their freedom to thrash vainly about, and follow someone who tells them what to do and where to go.[10]

If pigeons are desperate enough for food, they will do anything made available to them to get it.

The relevance to our concern with desirable human societies is that people will reward producers and politicians who most efficiently make available to them what they most deeply value. This book, to repeat, is an effort to persuade you to value most deeply a humanistic conception of desirability rather than a collectivistic or individualistic one. The logic of the analysis, of course, says that my effort is likely to succeed only to the degree that you are dissatisfied with your present values or perceptions; but one can do only what one can do.

Freedom and Minorities
Three distinct categories of people in any reasonably large and

---

[10] The importance of such a message is neatly adumbrated in a sign one sees occasionally on the walls of summer roadside stands on Cape Cod, and probably other places where bright college students are found: 'This life is a test. It is only a test. If this were a real life, you would be told where to go and what to do.'

Experience versus Understanding

complex society often become the foci of special concern with issues of freedom and justice. They often become objects of 'prejudice' and 'discrimination' or even a demeaning kind of patronizing condescension by members of a dominant category who tend to apply their own Procrustean cultural standards to everyone. Those prejudiced and discriminated against then often develop counter-cultural movements of liberation, and they and allies from the dominant group begin movements for cultural pluralism, multiculturalism, and political correctness in language and other cultural symbols. The United States in the 1980s and 1990s often seems absorbed in the culture wars that result.

The three categories typically raising such issues are:

> 1 People with genetic, congenital, or experiential physical or mental characteristics which intrinsically disable them from many activities and roles in the prevailing institutional structure (for example, the blind, deaf, crippled, or neurologically impaired, or mentally retarded).
>
> 2 Those with physical characteristics which arbitrarily bar them from many roles in terms of the peremptory standards applied (for example, their gender, race, sexual preferences, ethnicity, language).
>
> 3 People whose different locations in the social structure expose them to different experiences generating tastes, preferences, values, abilities, or expectations differing from the dominants' (for example, those with differing religious, regional, occupational, educational, or recreational subcultures).

Following the usual custom, I will refer to all three categories as 'minorities'.

Often, the minorities have learned the dominants' culture and agree with their standards. Most blind, deaf, and crippled people agree it would be much better not to be they. Some people in the 'arbitrarily disadvantaged' category – blacks, immigrants, women, homosexuals – similarly learn the dominant definition, agree that they are inferior, and wish they were

Culture and Freedom

otherwise. Or at least, many of them learn to accept their second-classness and even use it as a power base to gain favour with the dominants. Women, traditionally, have been the most vivid examples of this last accommodation, although 'Uncle Toms' and 'Aunt Jemimas' among blacks, and costumed Native Americans, are noticeable also. Children of immigrants, too, have often been eager to shed traces of the old ways and become indistinguishable from 'real Americans'.

Acceleratedly since the Second World War, however, the liberation and multicultural movements have challenged all the acceptance accommodations, and made it necessary to rethink many implicit, taken for granted, cultural assumptions. Arguments about the issues have usually pitted two sets of themes against one another. The individualistic themes of everyone for themselves and accepting one's lot in life without complaint are often pitted against both the sentiment of altruism and the other individualistic theme of equality of opportunity; and the melting pot theme of all subcultures blending into one homogeneous American culture, is often pitted against the 'rainbow' or 'mosaic' theme of many different subcultures living side by side in a variegated American culture. The opportunity in all this for separating thoughts from perceptions in a humanistic manner has rarely, if ever, been developed. I will develop it here.

MINORITY DEMANDS. In their newly evolved refusal to accept second-classness, minorities make three kinds of demands for change in the conventional rules of institutional games. One is the demand for integration, for elimination of arbitrary standards of exclusion from certain roles and privileges, and the substitution of only germane criteria of ability to perform the roles. Women demand access to traditionally male roles in fire and police departments; in the armed services, including combat roles; in executive positions in corporations and political positions in government; and so on. Racial and ethnic minorities make parallel demands; and new legal rules are adopted prohibiting all such discriminations.

A second kind of demand is often related to the first demand

Experience versus Understanding

for greater equality of opportunity; namely, the demand for special treatments to compensate for the disadvantages under which the minorities have had to labour. So long as their handicaps, whether biological or social, reduce their chances to succeed, opportunities to compete remain unequal. The prototype compensations are the special parking places and wheelchair ramps for the physically handicapped; special education for them and for slow learners or the blind and the deaf; and day care centres and maternity leave for working mothers. Affirmative action programmes, requiring employers to go beyond mere colour blindness (or gender blindness, physical blindness, and the like) to active pursuit of, and even preference for, minorities for hiring and promotion are a further step in this direction.

The third general kind of demand is more subtle and difficult but just as important symbolically. It is the demand for equality of respect; for general public recognition of the equal worthiness of the minority subcultures. It is not enough, minorities understandably say, to have equal access to housing or jobs; it is important to their self-respect to be regarded as equal in prestige and esteem, *as such; on the grounds of* their minority attributes. Understandably also, this is often the hardest of the minority demands for dominants to meet; for it often requires a radical restructuring of the latters' most basic beliefs and values. It can also generate considerable ambivalence, conflict, and confusion among the minorities themselves.

Further still, it can and often does lead to strident demands for recognition of the *superiority* of the minority and to shrill near-paranoid charges of racism and sexism almost as ends in themselves. Todd Gitlin has described and analysed this process in much detail in *The Twilight of Common Dreams: Why America Is Wracked By Culture Wars.*[11]

One of the questions that get raised in this context is a nice illustration of the fact with which we started: direct experiences are meaningless to humans; we need cultural definitions to tell us what they are and how to respond. When the definitions are unclear, we are at sea, and are likely to misunderstand one another.

[11] Henry Holt and Co, New York, 1996.

Culture and Freedom

Consider, for example, the question of when and how certain characteristics of minorities should be noticed favourably, noticed unfavourably, and not noticed at all? How should men, for example, decide when to compliment women on their dress or figures; when to object to what they see as exploitative use of their sex or feminine wiles, and when to ignore the facts of their femaleness? When should whites talk to blacks about their blackness in the way, say, they would talk to foreign tourists about their foreignness; when may they object to any perceived reverse racism, such as claims that all virtue stems from melanin; when should they guiltily submit to charges of historical discrimination; and when should they pretend they are unaware of race? When should able-bodied people notice the fact of others' crippledness, with what kind of solicitousness, and when should they ignore it?

The question gets further complicated by the probably inevitable tendency of some members of some minorities to reach for equality of respect with a kind of reaction-formation against low self-esteem, and claim superiority to the erstwhile dominants. When should women feminists assert the natural superiority of women and seek to ban books by dead white European males; and when should men accept the assertions as understandable over-reactions? (Or patronizingly indulge them?) For that matter, when should some women reject a radical feminist demand that all women be treated like men, and insist instead on their liberated right to dress and act as motherly nurturers, dress and act as luscious sex objects, or even proudly practise the traditional role of courtesan, call girl, or whore?

When is it merely lucid to speak of mental retardation; when should one carefully learn to say 'intellectually challenged' instead; and when is it merely legitimate free expression (rather than reactionary repression) to call such political correctness, ludicrous?

It all depends. It depends on the worldview you bring to bear on the phenomena; on what you declare people to be for.

The worldview of humanism declares them to be for the purpose of making their best contributions to the human

Experience versus Understanding

pursuits of human ideals, as producers and as appreciative audiences and consumers of the pursuits. Several implications relevant to the present discussion follow from that.

The first, as we saw earlier, is that corresponding to the duty to contribute what your empowerments permit, is the right to treatments (before, during, and after gestation and birth) that give you optimum power to contribute. When the reproductive, socialization, and educational institutions fail to give you such power, you have, humanistically, the right to indemnification for the failure – to compensation, remediation, correction. And you have the right to play all the institutional roles in which people make their contributions, that you have been empowered to play.

Of course, all irrelevant criteria for productive role-playing should be eliminated. *Of course*, members of the society who have not been disadvantaged owe recompense to fellow members they have allowed (through powerlessness, negligence, or wilfulness) to be handicapped, which is to say, relatively powerless. The opposite views are simply absurd, given humanistic premises – weird, outlandish.

For the same reasons, the handicapped owe to everyone the same things everyone owes to everyone. One of those obligations is to make the best contribution they can make. One of the claims some handicapped people make (and some people who are only narcissistic) is for support without reciprocal contributions, on the grounds of empathy, sympathy, pity, and altruism. But these are cons, as humanistically beyond the pale as any other kind of exploitation.

They are similar in that respect to some of the claims of other minorities for equal respect for their subcultures. To begin at an obvious extreme, a subculture calling, however genuinely and sincerely, for human sacrifice or sadistic rituals does not, humanistically, get equal respect. Nor do subcultures claiming the superiority of supernatural over scientific methods of understanding, or the superiority of magical over technological methods of coping, or the superiority of intuitive over due process methods of justice. Groups which insist that their subcultural preferences for leisure or occultism or many children or whatever do not permit them to contribute to a humanistic world or to live by humanistic rules should, perhaps, be respectfully left alone; but there is no humanistic duty to support them.[12] The irony of their claiming equal respect by appealing to humanistic values of reason and justice is interesting as a quaintness but not as morality or as a political reality.

We can summarize much of this chapter to this point by noting that, humanistically, if you choose to admit people into your society as fellow members, whether through birth or immigration (or conquest, as in the different cases of Native Americans and slaves), you incur the duty either to empower them or compensate them. You also incur the duty to respect them as equals by demanding of them the same things you demand of yourself: humanistic standards.

For that reason, it is simply humanistic rationality to be careful about whom you admit as members of your society, by either channel; but that is a matter for the next chapter.

Summary: The Theses of Chapter 8

Freedom and Privilege
Maximizing freedom is an oxymoron: within persons, freedom is limited by character; between persons, freedom is zero sum.

Markets and Democracies
Markets and democracies are protections against the operation of Lord Acton's dictum that power corrupts.

Four rules of the market: the 'free market' is a set of rules sharply *restricting* people's freedoms.

Four rules of democracy: democratic freedom is a set of rules sharply *limiting* people's freedoms.

People's Wants and Human Needs
That markets and democracies maximize control by consumers and citizens does not necessarily lead to a desirable society.

---

[12] See Chapter 10.

Experience versus Understanding

Freedom and Minorities
The zero-sum nature of freedom is nowhere clearer than in the case of minority rights and demands for various freedoms.

9

The Preciousness of Persons

The dictionary definition of 'individualism' is: 'the doctrine that the interests of the individual should take precedence over the interests of the state or social group.' Individuals are ends in themselves, more precious than any other entities; and everything else is for them and their interests. They are not 'for' anything outside themselves. For a person to be used, instrumentally, for something or someone else is always, from this point of view, a shocking idea, virtually a profanation.

To Whom Are Individuals Precious – and Why?
As stated, the doctrine is useless as a guide to action, because of the ambiguity of the idea of 'the individual'. *Which* individual? And *which* of his or her interests?

If it is to be a useful guide to action, individualism must be understood as telling each person to use every other person as an instrument for his or her ends; but that denies the idea that the other individuals are ends in themselves. That is, however, the understanding many people defend. It becomes the ecological conception of order discussed earlier. The dictionary definition becomes operationally altered to read that *each* individual should give whichever of *his or her* interests he or she chooses, precedence over the interests of *all the other members* of the state

121

Experience versus Understanding

or social group; and relative powers properly determine the outcome.

In that form it could definitely be a useful guide to action, in the sense of being a clear and unambiguous directive to each person;[1] but it leads, as we have seen, to the Tragedy of the Commons and the mutual destruction of Prisoners' Dilemma.

Viable societies that give lip service to the doctrine manage to survive in practice by none the less evolving rules that sharply limit individual freedom to follow it, as we saw in Chapter 8. As interdependencies become tighter, and various subgroups become more demanding about the precedence of *their* special interests, the rules proliferate and become ever more restrictive. It becomes necessary to build more prisons for losers who take seriously the idea of putting their own interests above the rules and get caught at it; and to provide ever more welfare subsidies to losers who feel too powerless even to be crooks. It becomes increasingly the case that many people become powerful enough not to get caught at giving precedence to their own interests in the form of graft, corruption, embezzling, insider-trading, tax evasion, misrepresentation, conning, lavish special interest lobbying, and the other 'scandals' which become the norm of the daily news.

Despite its problems, the doctrine of individualism is always defended against doctrines of collectivism on the ground that it is more devoted to the preciousness of individual lives. Compared to collectivisms, that is clearly a good defence, although it has a serious problem I will return to. In fact, however, the doctrine of humanism, which declares that individuals are temporary trustees of the species' gene pool and cultures and as such are for the welfare of humanity, is even more solicitous of the preciousness of individual lives. For it entails the principle that the state and all social groups and all their members *owe* to all individuals treatments which empower them to earn the self-respect that comes from competently making valued contributions to important ends.

---

[1] It requires, of course, unquestioning acceptance of each person's definition of his or her interests as whatever the powerful persons in her or his shaping environment had dictated.

The Preciousness of Persons

Some Classical Formulations of Humanism

Much of this is not new. The elements of humanism had been realized by several classical writers before. Sigmund Freud had written at the end of *Civilization and Its Discontents*:

> The fateful question for the human species seems to me to be whether and to what extent their cultural development will succeed in mastering the disturbance of their communal life by the human instinct of aggression and self-destruction ... And now it is to be expected that the other of the two Heavenly Powers, eternal Eros, will make an effort to assert himself in the struggle with his equally immortal adversary, Thanatos. But who can foresee with what success and with what result?

Emile Durkheim, the sociologist, had earlier put the same idea in less poetic and instinctual terms (1898; 1973: p 163). Society, he said:

> cannot be formed or maintained without our being required to make perpetual and costly sacrifices. Because society surpasses us, it obliges us to surpass ourselves; and to surpass itself, a being must, to some degree, depart from its nature – a departure that does not take place without causing more or less painful tensions ... Therefore, since the role of the social being (as distinct from the 'egoistic' being) will grow ever more important as history moves ahead, it is wholly improbable that there will ever be an era in which man is required to resist himself to a lesser degree, an era in which he can live a life that is easier ... To the contrary, all evidence compels us to expect our efforts in the struggle between the two beings within us to increase with the growth of civilization.

The severity of the struggle might be mitigated and civilization's side strengthened, Durkheim thought, if the concept of individualism were differently understood. In his view (1898;

Experience versus Understanding

1973: p 44), to think and act as individuals should not be to think anarchically, from the perspective of utilitarian egoism. It should be understood in the way I have been calling humanistic. That entails the understanding, as Durkheim put it, that 'duty consists in disregarding all that concerns us personally, all that derives from our empirical individuality, in order to seek out only that which our humanity requires and which we share with all our fellowmen.'

In *Demian*, Herman Hesse celebrates the importance of individuals in his emphasis on the fact that every person is a totally unique combination of molecules and experiences, never seen before and never to be seen again. As such, Hesse insisted, every person's story is 'important, eternal, sacred'.

At the same time, the humanistic perspective joins Adam Smith (better known as the intellectual father of capitalism but also the author of *The Theory of Moral Sentiments*, 1756; 1976: p 83) in rejecting the egoistic narcissism of individuals:

> We must ... view ourselves not so much according to that light in which we may naturally appear to ourselves, as according to that in which we naturally appear to others ... Though it may be true that every individual, in his own breast, naturally prefers himself to all mankind, yet he dares not look mankind in the face and avow that he acts according to this principle ... When he views himself in the light in which he is conscious that others will view him, he sees that to them he is but one of the multitude in no respect better than any other in it. If he would act so that the impartial spectator might enter into the principles of his conduct, he must ... humble the arrogance of his self-love and bring it down to something that other men can go along with.

The humanistic view is a view which at its best can enable us, as John Rawls says (1971: p 587), to see our place in the world *sub specie eternitatis*, from the perspective of eternity. By this Rawls means the ability

The Preciousness of Persons

to regard the human situation not only from all social but from all temporal points of view. The perspective of eternity is not a perspective from a certain place beyond the world, nor the point of view of a transcendent being; rather it is a certain form of thought and feeling that rational persons can adopt within the world.

Rawls added that 'Purity of heart, if one could attain it, would be to see clearly and to act with grace and self-command from this point of view.'

Saving and Spending Time and Persons
While purity of heart is a little much to hope for, a certain amount of grace and self-command seems a not unreasonable ideal. To approach it, we need the distancing from our immediate perceptions I have been emphasizing. In the present context, this means the humanistic understanding of individual lives as being like time: they cannot be saved, in any sense of 'saving them up'. They cannot be hoarded. *They have to be spent.*

There is no way not to spend them on some activity or another, and whatever activity is chosen will have consequences. It will make the world and the actor different, at least a little and sometimes a lot.

People speak of 'killing time'; and someone once asked, 'Who is slain when time is killed?' Humanistically, we know at least one answer: the person who would have existed if the time had been used differently. If you had played tennis instead of practising the piano those two hours, you would have been, however slightly, a different person; and so with all the weightier choices you have made and are making.

Lives, too, have to be either invested or wasted. They are different from time in that resources have to be invested in them if they are then to be invested in valuable activities; that is, activities having valued consequences. What consequences are valued?

Well, humanistically, as we have observed often, two kinds of consequences are valued: those consisting of contributions to

Experience versus Understanding

the species' understanding, technology, justice, and art (inspiration and catharsis); and those consisting of self-respect for the person, as producer and as appreciator of others' contributions.

If some individual lives are not the recipients of humanistic investments, they cannot be subsequently invested in either one of those activities. They are wasted. That waste of many lives is an inevitable consequence of the individualistic doctrine, which says, among other things, that if any investments are to be made in human lives, individuals must make them selfishly; that is, on the basis of a calculation that it is advantageous to *them*, individually.

You can run a society that way, at least for a while; but the costs go up, importantly because the waste is so great – quite apart from the individual suffering involved.

Humanistically, lives are so precious that it is a humanistic sin to further your individual welfare at the expense of other people. A cardinal limit on individual freedom is a commandment against externalizing the costs of your self-indulgence on to other people without their permission. A key instance is the humanistic attitude towards reproduction and, as a corollary, towards abortion.

The Plea of the Ovum
Detach your understanding from your immediate perceptions and habits of thought, and consider the perspective of an ovum, waiting anxiously, we shall imagine as a thought experiment, for its potential life as a human being to be determined. Can you conceive of its *not* making the following claim?

> I am obviously at your mercy. I have no power or bargaining power in relation to you. I can only appeal to the golden rule: please, for the sake of anything you hold sacred, treat me the way you would want to be treated if you were in my place.
>
> Try to give me the best equipment possible to enable me as a producer to contribute to the human enterprise, if only because the respect I'll get from others and the self-

The Preciousness of Persons

respect I'll have depend on my making valued contributions to important goals. Give me, as a consumer, the equipment to appreciate civilization's successes to date. I want to be able to see, hear, smell, feel, breathe, walk, run, jump, co-ordinate my muscles, learn, think, talk, write, read. And I'd like to be able to do those things for at least the average lifespan.

I realize that if you force me to become conscious as a person who does not have those attributes, I will probably prefer to live than to die, because the DNA you will force on me seems to work that way. But it would be cruel of you to coerce me into that situation. You could also enslave a person and then argue that slavery is moral because most slaves apparently prefer slavery to suicide; but I urge you to reject that obviously cheap way out.

If you get me fertilized into a foetus, and then incubate me all the way to birth, and then thrust me into the shaping environments that will shape me, you are coercing me into an existence you choose for me.

So, before I become a conscious 'me', I ask you please to create only a 'me' that will have the consciousness to which I have a humanistic right. If you insist on launching me into the world, let the me you launch be a me any rational person would choose to be. In case your mind happens to run in God terms, then for God's sake bear in mind that you cannot cop out on your responsibility by hiding behind God. It isn't God who would make me be born into a state no one would choose; it is you.

Therefore: have all the blood tests and genetic screening your culture makes available; screen the fertilizer of your ovum with equal care; avail yourself (and me!) of all the engineering possible; eat well and nutritionally; stay off drugs; don't smoke; don't create me if you can't provide for me; and abort this launch if you cannot do those things for me.

In short, please don't sacrifice me for your egoistic

Experience versus Understanding

desire to be a mother, or because of the pressures of people who urge irresponsibility on you.

Put summarily, the humanistic reply to such a plea is: 'You are right. We accept responsibility for providing you with the most empowering qualities and environments possible, and for holding you responsible for taking productive advantage of them.'

The individualistic reply is: 'You are wrong. By our rules you must take your chances with the qualities and environments chance gives you; and we will none the less hold only you personally responsible for the outcomes.'

We can summarize the humanistic view developed in this book so far, in a relatively few key intellectual understandings of the world that help to define it and underlie it; and a few policy principles that follow from the understandings – if you add the premise that the purpose is the ongoing welfare of the human species.

Key Understandings of Humanism

THE UNDERSTANDINGS
1 An actor's actions at any given moment are determined by certain controls inside the actor (such as genes or character).
2 Change and stability are governed by the principles of evolution, which are, at all levels, essentially: internal controls → action → external selection → internal controls → action → external selection → .

Corollaries:
1 The rules you enforce (external selections) determine the behaviour you get and in the long run the character (internal controls) of the persons from whom you get it. (NB: characters are *outcomes*.)
2 A's behaviour – very much including A's speech – tells you about A (his or her internal controls) and nothing else (except maybe the nature of his or her past environments).

The Preciousness of Persons

3 Everyone is capable of doing and believing anything at all, from the most base, vile, and stupid to the most elevating, inspiring, and brilliant. It all depends on how her or his character was formed.
4 To the degree that social institutions do not build desirable controls into people's characters, they must build them into people's environments.

3 Success in any undertaking is governed by power, which is determined by the degree of monopoly the actor has, either of what others need most and can pay for or fear most and can pay to avoid; and by the intensity of the actor's need.

Corollaries:
1 The outcome of the evolutionary principle of 2 above depends on the relative power of the actor and the selecting environment.
2 Your competition decreases your power; but other people's increases it.
3 The more powerful your clients, the more powerful are you.
4 You are better off than others to the degree that they were less lucky in the genetic and operant lotteries.

4 Bargaining power determines how little you have to pay for success; and its determinants are the same as those of power except that the less you want something, the greater your bargaining power, and the less your power.
5 One is responsible for outcomes one could have made otherwise.

Corollaries:
1 One is responsible for other people's lesser power to the degree that one could have made it otherwise.
2 One is responsible for one's own lesser power to the degree that one chose not to do the things that would have made it otherwise.

Experience versus Understanding

6 To evaluate people or performances you must have two things:

> 1 a conception of the purpose of the people or performances (which you cannot find; you can only declare it); and
> 2 comparative information, which requires competition (Wherein lies the advantage of markets and democracies over bureaucracies and dictatorships. See 10 below.)

7 The greatest significance of any action or event lies in its implications for the purpose of the largest system within which the actor shares interdependence.
8 Individual qualities (virtues, anguishes, joys) are independent of the desirability of actions. (Many Nazis were intelligent, heroic, despairing, and happy.)
9 Freedom cannot be maximized; it is zero-sum.
1 Among individuals, A's freedom to X precludes B's freedom from X.
2 Within an individual, character dictates, and no choice fails to cost many other choices. (And see 1 above.)

10 Markets and democracies are rules preventing the operation of Lord Acton's dictum. (They maximize corrective feedback to producers and rule makers, in accordance with consumers' values – which can easily be destructive of system welfare.)

> Corollary:
> The importance of 'free speech' is that the right of listeners to know of alternatives entails it.

11 The rational pursuit of their self-interest by subsystems, if successful, reduces the welfare of the system, and hence of the subsystems.

> Corollary:
> Societies whose members subordinate their personal

The Preciousness of Persons

welfare to the society's, as a result either of their characters or of their institutional mazes, are more viable than those whose members do not. (Ask any kidney; and cf. Prisoners' Dilemma and Tragedy of the Commons.

12 The preciousness of individual lives cannot lie in their being for themselves (they are too ephemeral by far); it lies in their being trustees of the human gene pool and cultures, and the only audience there is.

13 In the absence of shared premises from which to reason, conflict resolution requires either force or divorce.[2]

POLICY PRINCIPLES

The following policy principles are entailed by those understandings (given the premise that your purpose is the welfare of the largest system):

1 Concerning membership: Unrestricted exit; highly restricted entry. (Subsumes policies governing suicide and birth control; emigration and immigration; job leaving and job-seeking.)

2 Concerning freedom to act: No cost externalization not consented to (cf. Plea of the ovum – and of innocent bystanders).

> Corollary:
> The burden of proof should be on the person who would prevent other people either from obtaining something they want (eg, information), or from avoiding something they do not want inflicted on them (eg, children; bad art).

3 Concerning the purpose of life: Define it as the species' pursuit of improved adaptation, which requires ever-improved scientific understanding; art (catharsis and inspiration); technology; and justice.

4 Concerning the evaluation of people: Evaluate everyone in terms of their contributions to the purpose of life – both as producers and as consumers.

---

[2] The elaboration of this proposition is provided below.

Experience versus Understanding

5 Concerning the treatment of people:

> 1 Human lives are like time: they cannot be hoarded; they can only be used for this purpose or for that; or else wasted. Thus, to speak of 'sacrificing' rather than 'investing' them is usually to register disapproval of a certain use of them.
> 2 Everyone should be treated from before birth on so as to make their desirable potentials easier and more rewarding to them than their undesirable ones.
> 3 The costs of displaying the undesirable ones should be made greater and swifter than the benefits.

6 Concerning responsibility and security: if the reproductive, socialization, and opportunity institutions you support fail to assure everyone in your society the power to make valued contributions (rate well on the evaluations), then indemnify them for your failure – on condition of their conformity to the other policies.[3]

> Corollary:
> You cannot be responsible for the powerlessness of people whose relevant institutions you were powerless to control.

7 Concerning art[4] appreciation: good art is art which either clarifies the understandings or inspires the policy commitments, or is cathartic of[5] misunderstandings and policy wrong turns.[6]

The Physical and Moral Universes
We live in a physical universe governed by certain definite and

---

[3] This will put the great costs of inefficient and ineffective reproduction and socialization practices in the present, rather than in an apparently distant future, which is much better for concentrating the mind.
[4] All the arts: painting, literature, drama, dance, music, sports, entertainment – and conversation.
[5] Mocks, ridicules, derides, satirizes – or shows the tragedy of.
[6] If art is, instead, evaluated only in terms of its pleasingness to consumers (the subjective criterion) or to the artist ('for art's sake'), it is indistinguishable from crack.

The Preciousness of Persons

implacable laws. If you want an object to escape the Earth's gravitational force, you must give it a velocity of seven miles a second, which will require an amount of energy equal to one half the mass of the object times the velocity squared; and if you give it a velocity of less than five miles a second, the object will crash back to earth. Closely related is the fact we noted in Chapter 7: the ground holds you responsible for how you balance on your skates.

You have to conform to the laws of physics. Period. That's it. If you want the earth to rotate on its axis from west to east, you cannot have it. If you want to avoid influenza, you are more likely to succeed through immunization than through prayer. Those are the ways the world is.

Success in adapting to the physical universe lies in discovering what its laws are, and then learning either to give up any hopes that violate them, or to discover ways of realizing your hopes through conformity to them. If you are too stubborn for the former and not physically dextrous enough or technologically creative enough for the latter, you will skin your knees. Or worse.

If, then (admittedly, a very large if), there is to be a well-adapted human species extending into the future at least until the sun dies (and maybe, of course, even longer, somewhere else in the physical universe), two additional things will probably be necessary. One is to understand the corresponding laws of the human social universe, the ones summarized above as key understandings. The second is to *construct* a moral universe (that universe is not given to us) with laws of comparable implacability. The humanistic moral universe is outlined in the moral policy principles summarized above.

If the moral environment of people is such that those moral principles are both the necessary and the sufficient conditions for people to earn the respect of their fellows and self-respect, then we would have a humanistic society that could last handsomely for a long time.

If the moral universe does not consist of humanistic moral principles, there will still be a moral universe with laws comparable to those of the physical universe; it is just that they

Experience versus Understanding

will be different laws. That is, it will always be the case that if people act in certain ways, their environing other people will respond in certain ways; and those ways will be instances of the principles governing the society.

If the actually governing laws are such that humanistic principles are not *sufficient* for earning respect, we would have a society in which no matter how good you are, you might not get respect or feel entitled to self-respect. We would have a morally monstrous society inviting people desperately to try all the non-humanistic paths.

In any game, if you have been told that conformity to the rules is sufficient for you to be rewarded – or at least not punished – and you discover that that is a lie, you are likely to feel bitter, betrayed, alienated; and the rest of us should know better than to count on your continued co-operation. If you learn that they are not *necessary* for your success, you are likely to learn how to exploit the rest of us, by appealing to our pity or to our fear or gullibility. If you had thought such conformity was necessary for other people (legislators, for example), and you discover that that is not true, you are likely in addition to learn cynicism. You would be living in a morally idiotic society, one that breeds (selects out for reinforcement) attitudes and behaviour of exploitation, distrust, and mockery.

If the principles that would define a humanistic moral universe were neither necessary nor sufficient for respect, then we would have the anomic world that so terrified both Tony Kushner's antedeluvian prelapsarian Bolshevik and God's Angels.[7]

The Impossibility of Not Being a Moral Environment
We can put this another way by bringing several threads together in a final striking iron law of human existence. It is actually a corollary of the principle of responsibility. It is that no one can avoid being one or another of those kinds of environments to everyone else.

Your character plus your power are unavoidably such that the people around you learn that:

---

[7] See Preface.

The Preciousness of Persons

1 They will get what they want from you only if but always if they conform to humanistic principles (you are humanistic).

2 They will get what they want from you if they conform, but they can also get it without conformity (humanistically, you are a pushover).

3 They will not always or necessarily get what they want even if they do conform (humanistically, you are monstrous).

4 Moral principles have nothing to do with their success (you are amoral, so they may as well be also, because the world is either a crap-shoot or a jungle).

If your character is humanistic but your power or bargaining power is inadequate to require humanistic conformity from others, you are not morally responsible for their exploitativeness or amorality; only ineffective. If your power is adequate but you choose not to use it, you have chosen to foster non-humanism. There is no physical, chemical, or biological law preventing that; but there is an inexorable tragedy at the end of it, if there are very many like you. Those are the ways a humanistically moral universe is.[8]

The Place of Physical Force
The matter of power, independently of character or basic worldviews, is crucial in the evolution of human societies either towards or away from a humanistic world. Character or worldview, remember, determines how you will act, what you will try to achieve and how you will try to achieve it. To what degree you *succeed* is a matter of your power.

---

[8] An impressive example of the difference it makes what sort of environment you are, is provided by the strategy that has proved to be the winning strategy in Prisoners' Dilemma situations. It is called 'Tit for Tat'; and, in terms of the illustration used in the table on page 21 above, it consists, for Gretel, of first choosing Row 1 (the cooperation action), thus permitting Sam to gain 5 by choosing Column A; and *after that imitating whatever action Sam chooses*. Sam is now facing an inexorable environment in which he gains by cooperating and loses by not doing so. See Robert Axelrod (1984).

Experience versus Understanding

Ultimately, it is a matter of one particular basis of power: force. Coercion. Might.

We noted in Chapter 5 that the determinants of your power are your control over things that other people value, the number of such persons, the intensity of their wants or needs, the number of your competitors, and your willingness and ability to *use* the things you control – your power bases – to secure their compliance. One power base you might control is the physical force to coerce the others into doing what you want them to do, or at least to inflict such high costs on them for non-compliance that they decide compliance is a better deal.

In stable societies, force as a power base is legitimately a monopoly of the government; citizens are legally barred from using it. (If they use it anyway, the physical force of the government is used against them – in stable societies.) Governmental coercion is always there in the background, as the basis of the power for enforcing the institutional rules of the game, whether those rules are individualistic, collectivistic, or humanistic. It is another inescapable principle of human social life, which we need to add as our final key understanding of mature human beings:

> In the absence of shared premises from which to reason to a decisive conclusion, conflict resolution among interdependent people requires either force or the elimination of the interdependence; that is, divorce. (But even the divorce requires coercive enforcement, at bottom; and so do the shared premises.)

The adamantine nature of this fact of human social life deserves elaboration.

Fundamental Conflicts and Ultimate Purposes
I observed earlier that individual moral and/or instrumental virtues are irrelevant for evaluating the desirability of actions: saints and sinners are equally capable of courage, loyalty, intelligence, strength, and so on. Actions must be evaluated in terms of their (probable) *consequences*; and consequences

can be evaluated only in relation to some prior criteria of desirability. Desirable actions are ones that, from your point of view, contribute to your purposes; undesirable actions are ones that impede or thwart your purposes. Everything depends on what you think human beings and their actions are *for*.

As we have seen, all declarations of what they are for are just that – declarations. They do not follow from any empirical observations, and not from any logical procedures. They cannot be induced, and they cannot be deduced. They can only be declared; and it is the human necessity – the power and the glory, if you like, but above all the inescapable necessity – to declare them.

What you think you and others are for does not follow from anything, but everything follows from it. You have to judge the desirability of your and their actions by how likely they are to further the welfare of *something*: yourself or your family (tribe, business, political party, ethnic or religious group, nation). Or the human species. Either some subsystem of humanity, or the whole system.

As we have also seen, control of people's characters, free wills, or identities by cultural scripts proclaiming the primacy of any of those subsystems is in the long run ruinous. Not, to repeat, for any theological or otherwise mystical reason; but for the same sorts of reason that would ruin an organism if any of its component organs could further its own welfare at the expense of the organism. We would, correctly, refer to such an organ as pathological; but our correctness would follow only from our prior declaration that the organ was for the organism, not the other way around.

The immediate relevance of those reminders of understandings we have already gained, is to certain urgent questions of contemporary national and international politics. For example, how can we decide between the rival claims of Jews and Muslims for control over places (in Hebron, for example) genuinely sacred to each of them? Between the claims of Hindus and Muslims? Between Serbia and Croatia? Between poor Americans who want more government help and richer Americans who want lower taxes? Between American corporations who want to sell high tech equipment to Iran, and State

Experience versus Understanding

Department officials who want to isolate Iran from international commerce?

The relevance of the humanistic understandings we have gained is that we cannot. It is absurd even to think about trying, because the very premises of the disagreements flatly rule out *any* of the grounds on which one group or person can possibly get another to comply with the wishes of the first.[9] The possible grounds, recall, are to appeal to the others' altruistic compassion; to appeal to their self-interest by, in effect, buying them off; to appeal to a higher authority or some previously agreed-upon rule for deciding disagreements (majority vote, coin tossing, Supreme Court); and to appeal to some shared goal, for the sake of which it is plainly rational to act in one way rather than another. But in the (many many) kinds of cases mentioned above, the cultural scripts governing participants' perceptions and values mean that there *is* no compassion; it would be a betrayal of identity either to buy off the evil opponent or to be bought off; there is no previously agreed-upon decision rule or authority; and there is no shared goal.

It is a fundamental pathology of individualism: when two or more subsystems declare that they are ends in themselves and the others are either means or obstacles, there can be no answer to the question, How should we decide their dispute?

Except force.

All the foregoing considerations apply to the area of international relations, as well as to interpersonal ones, as we see in the next chapter.

Summary: The Theses of Chapter 9

To Whom Are Persons Precious – and Why?
For humanists, individuals are precious to everyone because they are trustees of the species' gene pool and cultures, and the only audience there is of the human drama.

Some Classical Formulations of Humanism

---

[9] Save one, coercion, which I will return to.

The Preciousness of Persons

Saving and Spending Time and Persons
Individual lives are like time: they cannot be hoarded; only invested, spent, or wasted.

The Plea of the Ovum
A thought experiment: every ovum pleads to be fertilized and born well, or else aborted.

Key Understandings of Humanism
The intellectual understandings that should, humanistically, guide interpretations of experiences are summarized in a few interrelated propositions.

The Physical and Moral Universes
Viable human societies need to construct a moral universe with principles as implacable as those of the physical universe.

The Impossibility of Not Being a Moral Environment
You cannot avoid being one kind or another of morally selective environment to people around you; but you may be one kind or another.

The Place of Physical Force
In the absence of shared premises, conflict resolution requires either force or divorce – and shared premises must ultimately be backed by force.

Fundamental Conflicts and Ultimate Purposes
When people's conceptions of what they are for consist of subsystems of the species, conflicts are resolvable only by force, if they are resolvable at all.

10

Foreign Policy

'Twas a famous victory, then, the end of the Cold War, but with victories like this, who could abide defeats? The formula for American commonality would have to be worked up and fought over anew.

Todd Gitlin[1]

It is not impossibly unreasonable to think of the United States as the society with the best chance of making itself into a moral universe for its members, and of leading the way for other societies to evolve towards humanism. 'The best chance' does not mean it will, or even that the chance is very great. Maybe the chance is so small it would be silly to bet on it. Americans changing themselves enough to create a moral universe is a staggering enough prospect,[2] and influencing such change over the planet is about as daunting as anything imaginable. Maybe it will never happen. If it happens at all, it will probably be at a glacial rate.

Meanwhile, not making any effort to make it happen reduces the chances a lot; and making efforts gives a point to life that is otherwise missing (unless you are an end in yourself or a fascist of one sort or another).

[1] *The Twilight of Common Dreams*, 1995.
[2] See note 4 in Chapter 7 about the agonies of change.

Experience versus Understanding

National and Personal Foreign Policy
Foreign policy is always a matter of deciding what 'the national interest' is in any given situation with respect to other nations, and then deciding what the best strategies and tactics are for furthering it. That is to say that 'foreign policy' for the collective actor, a nation state, is exactly like the policy of any individual actor facing other individual actors. Every person can readily be conceived as having a foreign policy towards everyone else. Everyone is always asking, more or less implicitly, 'What is my interest in relation to him or her or them, and how do I go about furthering it most efficiently?' And by 'interest', everyone always means the same general kinds of things: what, in the way of goods, services, information, or attitudes do I want to get from them; what do I want them to accept from me; what do I want to hold on to, keep away from them; and what do I want them to keep away from me?

In dealing with 'them', the options for all actors, whether individual or collective, are also the same: define them as irrelevant to the actor's own selfish (nationalistic) welfare and ignore them; define them as instruments or obstacles to it and try to use them accordingly; define them as objects of pity and sympathy who need altruistic help (or as Persons Bountiful who might take pity on oneself); or define them as actual or potential fellow co-operators in the long-run humanistic pursuit of species welfare.[3] The arguments for a humanistic definition over the others are the same in either case. (The Tragedy of the Common is the same tragedy whether the actors are Gretel and Sam or Germany and the United States. The dilemma of the Prisoners is the same whether it is you and I who are interdependent or our different countries.)

The big difference between individual-level foreign policy and national-level foreign policy is obviously the matter of sovereignty, which means simply the monopoly of legitimate

---

[3] The logical fourth alternative, which I labelled the collectivistic option in the case of individuals, would be an alliance of nations against some other alliance; but given planetary wide interdependence in the present day, I will not pursue this option. It has to reduce, now, to a temporary tactic in the pursuit of either nationalistic or humanistic purposes.

Foreign Policy

force within a specified area. Within all nation states, sovereignty was once a major issue also; but in most of the major modern ones, the issue has been settled. It was settled by force. England definitely lost the argument in the case of the American Revolutionary War, and the Southern Confederacy definitely lost it in the American Civil War; so now we have the sovereign nations of the United Kingdom and the United States, and not any sovereign nation of a Southern Confederacy. Those are all instances of the twelfth key understanding at which we arrived in Chapter 9: if there are no agreed-upon principles for resolving conflicts by reason, they must be resolved either by divorce or by force. And since divorce is practically impossible in a tightly interdependent world, that leaves force, if there is no common premise (ultimately backed by a monopoly of force) from which to reason.

So what should be the foreign policy of the United States under the present conditions of unavoidable interdependence with many other nations, and only widely varying shared premises, none of them enforceable by any common monopolist of force?

The question, obviously, covers all the international issues usually on the front pages of daily newspapers, which, to repeat, are the issues also headlined about internal domestic relations: foreign trade balances (domestically, who owes how much to whom?); barriers to foreign trade such as quotas or tariffs (domestically, who is discriminating against whom?); exchange rates (the bargaining power between parties); immigration and emigration policies (who is being and not being allowed into neighbourhoods or occupations, or prevented from leaving?); smuggling (black markets); nuclear proliferation (availability of hand guns); foreign aid (welfare payments); and, increasingly, the question of the use of force by the budding transnational monopolist, the United Nations, to intrude for various purposes on the sovereignty of individual nations (federal intervention in state, local, and individual rights).

As I write, the instances of that last issue that dominate the headlines are the cases of Bosnia in the former Yugoslavia, of

Experience versus Understanding

Iraq, and of Haiti. The debate over the proper foreign policy of the United States in such cases is usually couched in the terms of 'What national interests are at stake that warrant the risking of American lives in a military intervention?' (From strong opponents of American military intervention, 'How many American lives are you willing to sacrifice for that?')[4]

As you read, there will probably be other instances; but the fundamental issues, humanistically understood, are always the same. The most fundamental ones are the issues of what life is for, and the nature of individual or national moral responsibilities.

How Many Lives Should Be Risked?
Virtually any answer to the question, 'How many lives are you willing to sacrifice for ... (Bosnia, Haiti ...) seems too callous to utter.

The same question, of course, could be asked about almost any collective act – and is at least implicitly asked every day, and answered. How many American lives are we willing to sacrifice for law enforcement in the United States? Fire fighting? Permitting automobile transportation? Getting highway bridges built? Maintaining the American way of treating young black males?

Leaving to one side the political cynicism that often seems to motivate the question, the fundamental issue it raises deserves to be considered seriously. When is it justifiable to command people to act in a way that has a definite probability of their dying or (worse) being maimed in the action? Clearly, at least the following variables have to be weighed: the nature and value of the perceived benefit of the action; to whom it is a benefit; the probability of realizing the benefit by the action contemplated; the probability of the deaths; and the nature and value of the lives risked – first, to the risk-takers, and second, to their commanders.

Let us assume for the sake of this discussion that the people

[4] Usually pronounced 'for *thaat?*'

to be 'commanded' have voluntarily agreed to place themselves in roles in which they are subject to such commands. This is the case in a volunteer army, or even a draft army to the degree that citizens have agreed to the institution of a draft; and it is true in my examples of policepersons, fire fighters, car drivers, and bridge workers. (Would you say it is true of young American black males?)

Let us also assume for the sake of making the discussion illustratively concrete that the action we are considering is a military action; that the probability of success is .7; and that the probability of deaths among American soldiers (the estimated casualty rate) is .001. (That is, one death for every thousand soldiers each year.)

Next, consider 'the nature and value of the lives risked to the risk-takers.' Is it possible to think about this in any reasonable way? One position, of course, is that every life is an end in itself, and is priceless. This entails that no benefit is ever worth any risk to any life. It is a position that ends the matter.

In the *Iliad*, Homer has Patroklos express a different view, which may seem more appropriate to many people. 'If we had the option of living for ever, then we would take care not to risk our lives (the potential loss would be enormous); but since none of us will live for ever, the important thing is to live well and to bring glory to our lives before we die.' (I quote John Silber's paraphrase, 'Our Hellenic Heritage,' *Bostonia*, November–December, 1985, p. 27.) Much may depend on how we define 'glory' (more on that later), but in any case Patroklos's view indicates that not everyone thinks any risk is too great; so the matter has not ended yet. We need to reason further.

An important step is to recognize, as Homer did, that when we speak of 'a life' in this context we are actually speaking of something like 60 more years of living by (say) a twenty-year-old soldier. If we are thinking of 25,000 soldiers facing a casualty rate of .001, we are thinking about the probable loss of a tenth of a per cent of the life-years at stake. (Obviously, I am not dealing here with the enemy lives at stake; I come to them

Experience versus Understanding

later.) Is that too much? Is it a lot or a little? It is certainly a lot to the five persons, each of whom, we are assuming, will have lost sixty years of life, and to their friends and relatives. Is the probable benefit worth it *to them*? We must assume it is, since (we are assuming) they signed up for it. We do not even have to know why they signed up; that is, what benefits they foresaw as the result, to know that they thought the one in a thousand risk was satisfactory.

How about to the citizens whose agents (the President and Congress, let us say) issue the orders? How may we rationally think about the question of whether the spending of a tenth of a per cent of 1,500,000 life-years is a good or a bad idea for *them*?

(Bear in mind that the question, 'Who are they even to *think* about whether some benefit is worth other people's lives?' has already been answered. The established rules are that the Commander in Chief has the duty to make such decisions and the authority to do so; and our soldiers have declared that the benefit to them of risking such a decision is worth it to them.)

First, we must know what the potential benefit of the military action is.

We are comparing the erasing of 1,500 human life-years with the gain of something else; and I will assume agreement that the 'something else' has to be something vastly more important than any particular boundaries in Bosnia or the Middle East or putting any particular person in the presidency of Haiti. Since the '1,500 life-years' is a very general concept (we are not considering the concrete 60 years of John or Mary Smith's life, in which they might have had a good job and two wonderful children),[5] we should compare it with something equally general, and equally significant.

As I have emphasized, it is impossible to address such a task without some conception of what human lives are *for*. The answer that they are for themselves, intrinsically, is the answer that settles the matter, as noted above: *no* gain is worth that cost. If the matter is not to be settled so easily, we need to be

---

[5] Or have become paraplegics as a result of a hiking accident.

clear about how we, today, want to understand Patroklos's notions of 'living well' and 'glory'.

Whatever our specifications are, it must be understood that if we have any, they entail regarding human life-years as temporary present resources to be *spent* for something extending into the future – as, indeed, everyday speech clearly recognizes. We 'spend' our lives, or save them or waste them, and so on. We must think of them as resources to be *invested* in the production or maintenance of something beyond them, both in the sense of being in some sense 'more important' and in the sense of extending further into the future.

In any case, by itself, the answer that the life-years at risk are intrinsically priceless is clearly too shallow. It conceals the unavoidable other side of the issue: what will human lives be like *without* the risky undertaking? Without, for example, police forces, fire services, bridges, automobiles – or the contemplated military action? How many American lives are you willing to condemn to be spent in an undesirable condition?

Even short of the humanistic answer, there is an answer that I assume has enough meaning and appeal to everyone to let us continue the discussion. It is that, whatever else anyone may want lives to be for, they must be for the long-term maintenance of a social environment in which lives of adequate quality can be lived. That means, at the very least, an environment in which they and those to whom they owe duties live by the rule of law and are forbidden to use violence against weaker persons or groups for personal or parochial ends. Humanistically, we add to that minimum answer the claim that it means a moral environment institutionalizing the policies summarized in Chapter 9.

The question of whether the expenditure of 1,500 human life-years in a given undertaking is a good investment, then, is the question of deciding whether the social environment that will probably result from the investment is or is not more desirable than the environment that will probably result from not making it. The decision will make a difference for all the (vastly more) lives *not* invested. The question is, is the environment produced by not risking the tenth of a per cent, preferable in the

Experience versus Understanding

minds of the hundred per cent who will live in it, as compared to the alternative?

To Whom Do People Owe Duties?
That decision must be made, I said, on behalf of the decision makers themselves and 'all those to whom they owe duties,' particularly, in this context, the duty of guarding their future environment. To whom do people owe duties?

This is a terrible question, but one that must be confronted. No answer can be derived from science or logic. Like the answer to the question of what life is for, it can only be *declared* as an axiom. Those declarations do not derive from anything; but almost all other human decisions derive from them.

The minimum answer, I suggest, is that we owe duties only (but bindingly) to two general, but very definite, categories of people.

One is everyone *with whom we have entered some sort of social contract on behalf of the species*. This includes everyone in our own nation, and certain others I will come to. The second is everyone for whose existence we are responsible, such as our children and everyone in our society whose lives we have willed into existence by our support of the reproductive and socialization institutions which have produced them as they are.

Notice sharply that that conception says that we do *not* owe duties to two categories of people: those who have rejected our offer to join us in the humanistic contract; and those over whose life-shaping institutions we have no control, and therefore no responsibility.

That conception is significantly narrower than 'everyone alive', with dramatically different implications for action. Most significantly, it insists that the other persons whose future environments we undertake to protect must be persons *who are co-operating with us in that undertaking as evidenced by their current actions*. (People in our own society who are not co-operating in that project are still our responsibility because their non-co-operation must result from the way our reproductive and socialization institutions have so far operated to produce them the way they are.)

We do not owe duties to peoples in other nations who have not themselves developed social institutions which insist on the democratic rule of law and prohibit violence among themselves and against their neighbours. That does not mean that we should never use military action on their behalf; that depends on whether doing so contributes to the environment of those to whom we *do* owe duties.

What duties do we owe them? Whatever we have contracted for; but at the minimum, protection of their social environment *when the power we have available reasonably promises success.* It is plainly a ridiculous waste of resources, including lives, to invest them in undertakings when the probability of failure is great, as it is plainly both ridiculous and odious not to invest them when the probability of success is reasonable. The humanistic duty is to do what you can to advance humanism; it is not to commit suicide, or waste other people's lives, pointlessly.

Actions which promise to protect social environments guaranteeing the rule of law are, most fundamentally, actions which make breaches of that rule costly. Preferably, so costly that breachers find any hoped-for benefits not worthwhile. That is why, for example, bombing strategic targets of violators from the relative safety of the skies or from ships off the coast may often be the sanest action available; and protests about 'cowardly refusals to send ground troops' are simply irrelevant. The name of these games is not to risk lives; it is to protect humanistic environments, at as little cost to the protectors as possible.

It may seem that the reasoning I am suggesting is more complex and cumbersome than the customary formula, 'Is an action in the national interest?' but the emptiness of that formulation should be apparent. The question is, what *is* the national interest – to invest in producing and maintaining a lawful social environment, or to invest in one in which the rule is, 'Use violence when you can get away with it'? Either decision is an investment, and both will cost human life-years.

Experience versus Understanding

You cannot decide not to spend lives; you can only decide what to spend them *on*.

If you do not spend them on a good environment for the people you owe, you spend them on a poor environment for the people you owe. No law of nature dictates the choice; but a law of logic dictates that the choice you make reveals the character you have. Patroklos had it right.[6]

Daring to Take the Lives of Enemies
Even if you accept the foregoing reasoning about risking your own life, or the lives of your countrymen, there remains for some people the question, How do you dare take the lives of enemies?

The answer depends, as always, on what you think they are for. If, as would seem to be the pure pacifist position, you think they are so sacred as ends in themselves that the very question is sacrilegious, then you must think that the answer is simple: you do not dare to take the lives of enemies. You prefer to condone the violence they practise to the violence that would prevent it, and the loss of the lives of their victims to the loss of their lives. That is not a position that is assailable by logic or science. Like any other such declaration, it cannot follow from anything, but everything follows from it.

From the very different humanistic declaration, very different implications follow. If the enemy lives are hazardous to humanistic environments, entailing the loss of lives committed to humanistic values, then you dare to take them because the alternative is to let them destroy humanistic lives. Again, we are not offered by the world the option of only saving lives; we are often required to choose *which* lives.

The issues here are often phrased in the (usually negative) terms, 'Do you want the United States to be the world's policeman?' The humanistic answer has to be that it would be

---

6 Patroklos's counterpart is Shakespeare's Falstaff: 'Can honour set-to a leg? No. Or an arm? No. Or take away the grief of a wound? No... What is honour? A word... Who hath it? He that died o' Wednesday. Doth he feel it? No... Therefore, I'll none of it: honour is a mere scutcheon.' (*Henry IV, Part 1*, act 5, Sc. 1)

Foreign Policy

hard to conceive of a nobler role than that of policing a humanistic environment for human beings.

Investing in Nations

But at least one equally noble role can be conceived. It is that of investor in the humanistic environment of foreign nations which are losers in an ecological world of individualistic/nationalistic values.

The problems for the United States in this context correspond to those of affirmative action and compulsory education within the country. Here, though, they are usually discussed in the vocabulary of national sovereignty and the preservation of native cultures, versus western cultural imperialism and economic exploitation. The trouble with that vocabulary is not that it is always, or even often, inaccurate, and not that the moral concern it reflects is necessarily unjustified. The trouble, rather, is that it contains no useful clues about how to correct the situation. It is frequently a howl of protest, or sometimes a snarl, but neither a diagnosis nor a recipe.

First World–Third World or North–South relations are vivid examples of the dilemmas created when we contemplate bringing into one humanistic insurance pool two sets of people who have lived so far in such radically different cultures: First-World people in enabling and encouraging conditions; Third-World people in disabling and discouraging ones. The very hard fact at the present point in cultural evolution on the planet is, as we have said about underclass individuals in the United States, that the reason people in the Third World are so poorly off is that they lack power. And to lack power is, always, to be unable or unwilling to do anything that would cause First-World people to do more for Third-World welfare.

Third-World culturally scripted ways of life entail rates of population reproduction and levels and modes of economic production that generate the power and bargaining power in relation to the First World that they generate. No howls are going to change that. The situation here, moreover, is in a way more painful than the corresponding inequalities within the United States because here it cannot be said that the relatively

Experience versus Understanding

well-off population is responsible for the powerlessness of the poor, by virtue of supporting the social institutions that make them poor. The cultural rules of poor countries are their cultural rules, not ours. To say that those ways of life should not be changed, or that western efforts to change them amount to cultural imperialism, is certainly legitimate; but it is also certainly to say that the poor nations should remain poor (or, possibly, dependent wards at the mercy of western altruism).

True, the values or conditions of developed nations might change so that the offerings of poor nations become valued, with no changes on their part. Western industrialism's need for oil transformed some Middle Eastern nations from very poor to very rich very fast. For present purposes, however, it does not seem wise to hope for much in that direction.

That means helping to provide the educational, technological, political, and administrative resources necessary to be competitive in the modern world economy; and it means insisting on the understandings and policies summarized in Chapter 9. It probably means sending steadily for decades and decades to come something along the lines of the following message:

> We will invest at no interest a rising percentage of our national income up to one per cent (as recommended by the United Nations) to support, but only to support, actions on your part which succeed, at the same rate, in lowering your rate of population growth and raising your rate of economic productivity until you achieve equality with us. If it is too sad or too hard for you to change your way of life to do that, we respect your right to make your own choices. Get in touch if you change your mind. The offer always stands. In the meantime, we say to you what we say to our own members: so long as you accept all the costs of your present life styles, you are welcome to them; but any elements of your character or culture which endanger the environments of people to whom we owe duties are, so far as our power permits, no longer respectable on this planet.[7]

---

[7] Dictators and racists of the world, take note.

Foreign Policy

Summary: The Theses of Chapter 10

National and Personal Foreign Policy
The issues of national foreign policy parallel those of each person's policy towards other peoples.

How Many Lives Should Be Risked?
If individuals are only for themselves, international force cannot be justified; but if they are investable in something else, it can be. But risking lives in war or peace-keeping operations requires weighing the value of investing human life-years for one set of consequences against risking them for another set.

To Whom Do We Owe Duties?
We owe duties to everyone with whom we have contracted and to everyone whose lives we have, one way or another, willed into existence; but not to others.

Daring to Take the Lives of Enemies
Destroying enemy lives is justified if not doing so will destroy the humanistic welfare of people to whom we owe duties.

Investing in Nations
Humanistically, we owe to less developed nations investments in humanistic environments for their members, contingent on their subscribing to humanistic values.

Bibliography

Ackoff, Russell L and Fred E Emery, 'On Ideal-Seeking Systems', *Yearbook of Society for General Systems Research*, vol. 17, 1972, pp. 17–24.
Adam, J Stacey, 'Equity Theory Revisited' (with Sara Freedman), in L Berkowitz and Elaine Walster (eds), *Advances in Experimental Social Psychology*, vol. 9 (New York: Academic Press, 1976).
Asimov, Isaac, 'Nothing for Nothing', in *The Winds of Change* (New York: Dell Publications, 1984).
Axelrod, Robert, *The Evolution of Cooperation* (New York: Basic Books, 1984).
Beedham, Brian, 'What Next for Democracy?', *The Economist*, September, 1993.
Brim, Orville, 'Attitude Content Intensity and Probability Theory', *American Sociological Review*, 20: 68–76 (1956).
Deak, Istban, 'The Incomprehensible Holocaust', *The New York Review of Books*, September 28, 1989, pp. 63–72.
Doctorow, E L, *The Waterworks* (New York: Random House, 1994).
Durkheim, Emile, 'The Dualism of Human Nature and Its Social Conditions', in Robert N Bellah (ed), *Emile Durkheim on Morality and Society* (Chicago: University of Chicago Press, 1973).
Fish, Stanley, *There's No Such Thing as Free Speech ... And It's a Good Thing Too* (New York: Oxford University Press, 1994).
Freud, Sigmund, *Civilization and Its Discontents* (New York : W W Norton, 1961).
Fromm, Erich, *Escape from Freedom* (New York: Holt, Rinehart, and Winston, 1941).

Experience versus Understanding

Gitlin, Todd, *The Twilight of Common Dreams* (New York: Henry Holt and Co, 1995).

Goffman, Erving, 'On Cooling the Mark Out', *Psychiatry*, 15: 451–63, 1962.

Golding, William, *Lord of the Flies* (Faber & Faber. New York: Coward-McCann, 1962).

Hallie, Philip, *Lest Innocent Blood Be Shed* (New York: HarperCollins, 1994).

Hesse, Hermann, *Demian*, Harper and Row, 1965.

Homans, George C, *Social Behavior: Its Elementary Forms* (New York: Harcourt Brace Jovanovich, 1974).

Kelsen, Hans, *General Theory of Law and State* (New York: Russell and Russell, 1945).

Kuhn, Alfred, *The Logic of Social Systems* (San Francisco: Jossey-Bass, 1974) and *Unified Social Science* (Homewood, Illinois: Dorsey Press, 1975.

Kushner, Tony, *Angels in America, Part Two: Perestroika* (New York: Theatre Communications Group, 1994).

Lewontin, R C, 'Genes, Environments, and Organisms', in Robert B Silvers (ed), *Hidden Histories of Science* (New York: New York Review of Books, 1995).

Long, Norton, 'The Local Community as an Ecology of Games', *American Journal of Sociology*, 64: 251–61, November, 1958.

Nozick, Robert, *Anarchy, State, and Utopia* (New York: Basic Books, 1974).

Powers, William, *Behavior: The Control of Perceptions* (Chicago: Aldine Publishing Co, 1973).

Rawls, John, *A Theory of Justice* (Cambridge, Mass.: Harvard University Press, 1971).

Rorty, Richard, *Objectivity, Relativism and Truth: Philosophical Papers* (Cambridge University Press, 1991).

Schelling, Thomas, *The Strategy of Conflict* (New York: Oxford University Press, 1963).

Skinner, B F, *Science and Human Behavior* (New York: Alfred A Knopf, 1953).

Smith, Adam, *The Theory of Moral Sentiments* (edited by D D Raphael and A L Macfie, Oxford: Clarendon Press, 1976).

For Product Safety Concerns and Information please contact our EU
representative GPSR@taylorandfrancis.com
Taylor & Francis Verlag GmbH, Kaufingerstraße 24, 80331 München, Germany

www.ingramcontent.com/pod-product-compliance
Lightning Source LLC
Chambersburg PA
CBHW061839300426
44115CB00013B/2446